SPIRITUAL SURVIVAL IN THE LAST DAYS

Greg Laurie

HARVEST HOUSE PUBLISHERS
Eugene, Oregon 97402

SPIRITUAL SURVIVAL IN THE LAST DAYS

Copyright © 1982 by Harvest House Publishers
Eugene, Oregon 97402
Formerly *Occupy Till I Come*

Library of Congress Catalog Card Number 82-081-919
ISBN 0-89081-320-5

Printed in the United States of America.

FOREWORD

Greg Laurie was one of the Jesus People who came out of the hippie drug culture. He is now the pastor of a large church, attracting thousands of young people each week.

The hippie era was marked by an irresponsibility that grew out of despair. A despair for a world corrupted by its vain pursuit of happiness, focused on material things that could all be instantaneously dissolved by the Bomb.

That same irresponsibility is sometimes manifested by Christians today in anticipation of the soon return of Christ. I hear of those who dropped out of school, or hurried to get married, or even gave up promising careers, all predicated upon His soon return.

The command of Jesus to "occupy till I come," was intended to keep us from any rash or foolish act premised upon His soon coming.

With the increased interest in fulfilled Bible prophecy and the hope of the imminent return of Jesus Christ, it is more important than ever that we give careful consideration to His command, "occupy till I come."

As the pastor of thousands of young people, many of whom are thinking of altering their life's goals in anticipation of the Second Coming, Greg is highly qualified to encourage us to establish Biblical priorities in the last days.

Chuck Smith
Pastor, Calvary Chapel of Costa Mesa

CONTENTS

Foreword

SPIRITUAL SURVIVAL IN THE LAST DAYS

Greg Laurie

Chapter
1

1
Preparing Till He Comes

As you read this book there are developments taking place that show with incredible accuracy that prophecies made thousands of years ago by Hebrew prophets and by the Lord Jesus Christ are now being fulfilled. Our conclusion must be that the coming of the Lord is near, very near.

I recently had the opportunity to visit Israel and stand on the very mountain where Jesus gave one of the most stirring messages he ever uttered: the Olivet Discourse, recorded in Matthew 24. In this response to the disciples' question regarding the sign of His coming and the end of the world, Jesus described the last-days scenario that you and I are seeing and have yet to see, very possibly within our lifetimes. Jesus described the coming world leader who would deceive many people with his new economic system and personal charisma, and who would be energized by Satan himself.

Jesus described the Great Tribulation, that coming time of peril to the earth in which God will bring judgment to this world resulting in cataclysmic changes on the earth. In this sermon from the Mount of Olives Jesus described the rise of false religions and self-supported messiahs that would be rampant in the final days. Perhaps most dramatic of all, Jesus described the return of the Jewish people to their homeland of Israel after having been scattered for over 19 centuries to the four corners of the earth.

No More Joke

There was a time when the message of the coming of the Lord was carried by a bearded man carrying a sandwich placard and walking down the street saying, "The end is near!" But today, it is no longer a joke. The military leaders are telling us that things are coming to an end. The ecologists are telling us that we are destroying our natural resources. The lawmakers are telling us that crime is at epidemic proportions, with no end in sight.

The real focal point of the last-days scenario is found in the Middle East. The tiny land of Israel, in bringing the Jewish people back together into their land after being spread throughout the world for thousands of years is fulfilling the prophecy of Jesus in Matthew 24:32-34: "Now learn the parable from the fig tree: when its branch has already become tender, and puts forth its leaves, you know that summer is near; even so you too, when you see all these things, recognize that He is near, right at the door. Truly I say to you, this generation will not pass away until all these things take place" (NASB). The fig tree is symbolic of the nation of Israel which has budded again. This is what Jesus was prophesying. He said that the generation that saw this event happen would not pass away until all these things were fulfilled. "These things" refer to the events of the last days and the coming of the Lord. We have seen the fig tree bud as Israel has been regathered and established in her land. As Psalm 102:16 says, "When the Lord shall build up Zion, He shall appear in His glory." I have had the opportunity to visit Israel many times, and each time I have seen how the Jewish people have taken land that was a barren desert and cultivated and nurtured it into a land that is plush with greenery and produce. Most important of all, it is now a place where the Jewish people can live without fear of discrimination and persecution.

Attack on Israel

Not only did Jesus tell us that the people of Israel would be regathered in their land, but Scripture also tells us that a large force from the uttermost parts of the north will move on the tiny land of Israel in an unprecedented attack with the purpose of wiping her off the face of the earth (Ezekiel 38). As we study these Scriptures, we find that this large force is none other than Russia, which now has many motives for moving upon the land of Israel. One of the most notable of these is that the Syrians and Israelis have been at odds with each other for many years, and the Soviet Union has recently signed a 20-year friendship agreement with Syria guaranteeing to watch out for her and to militarily intervene on her behalf in the event of a confrontation.

If Syria and Israel were to get into an open war, this could easily bring in the Soviet Union. The Russians are building a circle of military power around the Persian Gulf right now and are tightening that hold more each day. There are many motives that could cause the Soviet Union to move, but one thing is certain: She will move eventually.

What It Means to You

You may be thinking, "What does all this mean to me?" What it means to you is that, when the Soviet Union and her allies move upon Israel, God is going to supernaturally intervene and deliver Israel out of their hand. Scripture tells us that God will wipe out five-sixths of the invading army.

After He performs this great and miraculous intervention, he will once again pour out His Spirit on the house of Israel. Romans 11:25 says, "Blindness in part has happened to Israel, until the full gathering of the Gentiles be come in." This spiritual blindness that rests upon Israel today will continue until all those people who are being gathered into the church are removed from the earth. Then the Spirit of God will be poured out upon Israel.

By and large the Jewish people have yet to recognize Jesus Christ as their Messiah; most still believe that He is yet to come the first time, much less the second. Yet in that day when Israel is attacked by the Soviet Union, with all the odds stacked against her, God will intervene on her behalf. The Lord tells us in Zechariah 12:9,10, "It shall come to pass in that day that I will seek to destroy all the nations that come against Jerusalem. And I will pour upon the house of David and upon the inhabitants of Jerusalem, the spirit of grace and of supplications; and they shall look upon me whom they have pierced, and they shall mourn for him, as one mourneth for his only son, and shall be in bitterness for him, as one that is in bitterness for his firstborn." So the Jewish people will recognize Jesus as their Messiah, and that long-standing spiritual blindness of the Jewish people concerning their Messiah will be lifted.

The Father's Many Mansions

Jesus said in John 14:2,3, "In my Father's house are many mansions; if it were not so, I would have told you. I go to prepare a place for you. And if I go and prepare a place for you, I will come again, and receive you unto myself, that where I am, there ye may be also." This is one of the greatest promises ever made. Jesus tells us He will come again. This is our hope and comfort—not so much the removal of the church from earth but rather the fact that we are being removed to heaven! My hope is not as much in the coming of the Lord as an event as in the person of the Lord who is coming. Jesus is coming to receive you to Himself; he's coming to deliver you from this earth and to take you to be with Him forever.

As we see these events happening in the Middle East, as we see these prophecies being fulfilled, as we see the imminent revealing of the Antichrist, it should bring in our hearts a sense of great anticipation.

If you are not a Christian, it may bring fear to your

heart. When you hear the message of the coming of the Lord, it may be something that frightens you rather than excites you. That's because you have not made proper spiritual preparation for it. The only proper preparation that can be made for the coming of the Lord is to have a living, vital relationship with Jesus Christ on a day-to-day basis. If you have that, you have nothing to fear; you can lift your head and look up, "for your redemption draweth nigh." If you don't have that relationship, a time of great judgment is coming upon the earth and upon you. I strongly encourage you to get ready to meet the Lord.

Busy Christians

As we realize that these things are going to happen, there are certain things that we as Christians should be doing. The purpose of this book is to look at what God tells us we should be doing as we wait for the return of Jesus Christ to the earth.

We can get so excited about Jesus' return that we disregard all our responsibilities and simply sit on the rooftops waiting for His return to get us out of this mess. Some Christians, sensing the soon return of the Lord, might go out and use their credit cards to charge up lots of items that they hope they'll never have to pay for.

Some people criticize those of us who believe that Jesus could come at any moment. They accuse us of putting all our hope in our "great escape" and of not dealing realistically with the world around us in reaching others for Christ (and, if calamity comes in not preparing for it). If this is the case with a believer (all his hope in the coming of the Lord rather than in the Lord who is coming), this is an unhealthy balance. There are certain important things we need to be doing as "last-days" believers.

Yet there is also a great danger in believing that the coming of the Lord is *not* near. In Luke 12:54,56 Jesus said in effect, "When you see a cloud is coming you say a shower is coming . . . You can interpret the weather but can't interpret *this* time."

Some people today are saying, as the Apostle Peter predicted, that the Lord is delaying His coming. I believe that if a Christian understands the teaching of the soon coming of Jesus to the earth *properly,* it actually motivates him to get busy doing what God wants him to do, because the time is short. This hope of Jesus' return should also have a purifying effect on a believer's personal life; as the Apostle John put it, he should "purify himself as God is pure" (1 John 3:3).

Chapter 2

2
Responsible Till He Comes

Jesus, speaking of His coming back to the earth, said in Matthew 24:37-42, "As the days of Noah were, so shall also the coming of the Son of man be. For as in the days that were before the flood they were eating and drinking, marrying and giving in marriage, until the day that Noah entered into the ark, and knew not until the flood came, and took them all away, so shall also the coming of the Son of man be. Then two shall be in the field; the one shall be taken, and the other left. Two women shall be grinding at the mill; the one shall be taken, and the other left. Watch therefore, for ye know not what hour your Lord doth come."

Jesus was speaking of His coming again to earth to remove the church in the rapture to be with Him. He pointed out that conditions in the last days would be parallel to the conditions in the time of Noah, prior to the flood.

The Dark Times of Noah

As we look back at the life of Noah we see that he was truly a last-days believer. He was living in a very dark time in human history. The only time comparable historically to that time is the time we live in now. The only difference is that Noah was a last-times believer waiting for the coming of the *flood* while we're last-times believers waiting for the coming of the *Lord*.

As we look back into the book of Genesis, we see the account of the times in which Noah lived, and we find many startling parallels to the time in which we live now.

Genesis 6:1 tells us that during the time of Noah men were multiplying on the face of the earth, and Jesus said that it would also be this way before His coming. We are seeing a multiplication of people as never seen before—a literal population explosion. The growth of man has been so remarkable over the years that we have practically outgrown our planet. In 1860 there were 1 billion people on the face of the earth; in 1930 there were 2 billion; in 1965, 3 billion; in 1970, 4 billion; and by the year 2000 there will be 6.5 billion people on earth!

As our population grows, especially in the underdeveloped countries, the earth is not able to provide food for all these people. A report was given to former President Carter on what the world would be like in the year 2000. The findings were called "Global Report 2000." This report noted that if present trends continue, the world in the year 2000 will be more crowded, more polluted, less stable ecologically, and more vulnerable to disruption than the world we live in now. The population will actually be growing faster in 2000 than it is today. The number of malnourished people could grow from 600 million to 3 billion. (Our total current population now is a little over 4 billion.)

Sexual Perversion

Another of the conditions in Noah's time was sexual perversion. There was an attempt by fallen angels to cohabit with earth women and produce a perverted version of the human race. The time in which we live right now is also a time of incredible perversion of sex. As we look around us right now, we see pornography growing in epidemic proportions.

Not only is sexual perversion growing in the area of unlawful acts between men and women, but it is growing in areas such as child pornography. I read recently of commercial enterprises involving children as young as three years of age! Three hundred thousand children are being victimized by pornography at any given moment, and they are being augmented by 60 to 70 thousand new children each year! There are some 260 magazines featuring juvenile sex scenes illustrated by photographs of young boys and girls involved in a variety of provocative poses and sexual activities.

One of the leaders of the pornographic industry said he believes the sex business has the same potential for sales and profit as the food industry. Over 5 billion dollars is spent on legal sex in the U.S. each year. In Times Square alone 1 billion dollars is spent each year!

We see society's acceptance of things that God has strictly condemned in His Word, such as homosexual activity. Romans 1:24,25 tells us that God gives people up to uncleanness through the lusts of their own bodies, to dishonor their bodies between themselves, because they changed the truth of God into a lie and worshiped the creation (the human body) more than the Creator. For this cause God gives people up to shameful lusts.

God is not condemning these people to a life of never knowing Him; He is offering forgiveness, but they must come and find that forgiveness at the cross of Jesus Christ. God loves the homosexual, but He doesn't want to leave him that way. God loves the adulterer; He loves the murderer; He loves the thief. He loves every human being, no matter what he or she has done, but again let me emphasize that *He does not want to leave them that way.*

Genesis 6:5 says that during the time of Noah the imaginations of man's heart were very wicked, and his thoughts were evil continually. It seems like everything that man thought was only taking him deeper and deeper into his sin. Romans 1:21 tells us that their imagination and thinking became futile and that their foolish hearts were darkened, so that even though they claimed to be wise, they were really just fools.

Epidemic of Violence

Another sin during the time of Noah was an epidemic of violence. Genesis 6:11 says, "The earth also was corrupt before God, and the earth was filled with violence." Right now we are seeing an epidemic of crime that is unparalleled in history. We also read in Scripture that in the last days we will be living in satanically energized times, and that men will actually go from bad to worse.

Not only are we seeing violent crime rising, but we're seeing it spread to people that we would never expect to be involved in violent crime. The *Los Angeles Times* recently carried a story describing a gun-toting children's army which is prowling the city streets and is programmed to kill. A juvenile court judge said recently, "I see kids packing .38 caliber revolvers and magnums and shotguns." This judge went on to tell a board of supervisors, "It's incredible. What I've observed is a children's army out there. I even had a defense attorney say to me, 'What on earth is going on out there? It's almost like they're programmed robots on the prowl to kill.' " Our court systems are not really able to handle this rise of crime. Teenagers account for one-third of violent crime arrests in Los Angeles alone. According to crime statistics, the number one criminal is between the ages of 15 and 20.

Unlikely Risks?

Not only are the young people turning to violent crime, but women are also becoming more involved. In the last 20 years the number of women arrested for violent crimes has gone up 300 percent! Women are now turning to crime three times faster than men. Looking at these horrible things that are taking place, it causes us to recoil in horror. One statistic states that every 24 minutes a murder is committed in the United States, every seven minutes a woman is raped, and every week 400 Americans are murdered. During one recent year, 110,000 teachers were injured in attacks on school campuses, and ten times that many students were assaulted!

It seems that the only safe place is in the home. Yet of the 47 million married couples in the United States, approximately 1.7 million have gone after each other with guns or knives! California statistics show that one-third of all females who were murdered were killed by their own husbands. About 70 percent of all assault victims cared for in hospital emergency rooms were spouses who had been attacked by a husband, a wife, or a lover.

As we see this rise of violent crimes in the world around us, we wonder what's going on. There is such a rapid rise in terrorism and assassination attempts that no one seems to be safe any longer. The ultimate fear among many experts now is that one of these terrorist organizations will get hold of a nuclear bomb, and instead of holding a group of people hostage they could hold an entire city hostage. Even as violence characterized the time of Noah before the flood, so violence characterizes our planet as we await the Lord's return.

How Noah Survived

How did Noah survive in such a godless time? The book of Genesis gives us one of the insights into

Noah's life: *He walked with God.* This is an expression that many people don't really understand. "Walking with God" means that we walk in the direction that He walks. This generally is not the direction in which the bulk of people around us are walking. Instead, they are walking in the broad way that leads to destruction. The Bible says, "There is a way that seems right unto a man, but the end thereof is death" (Proverbs 16:25). But God's people are to be walking the narrow road that leads to life. If we're going to be walking with God, it means that we can't walk with those who are going in the opposite direction.

Psalm 1:1 tells us, "Blessed is the man that walketh not in the counsel of the ungodly, nor standeth in the way of sinners, nor sitteth in the seat of the scornful." It seems that when we begin *walking* with the wrong people, soon we're *standing* with them, and then we're *sitting* with them. First we're moving and walking with them, then we're standing listening to them, and the next thing we know we're one of them, sitting in the seat of the scornful.

If we want to be like Noah as a last-days believer and to live right before the Lord, we need to walk with God. Scripture says that as a result of Noah's walk with God he was a just man and perfect in his generation (Genesis 6:9). This doesn't mean that Noah lived a flawless life, but rather that he was growing in his relationship with the Lord. Someone once said, "The Christian life is like a greased pole—you're either climbing or you're slipping." It's a constant effort as we seek to follow the Lord.

Noah's Secret

The book of Hebrews gives us the secret of Noah as a last-days believer: "By faith Noah, being warned of God of things not seen as yet, moved with fear, prepared an ark to the saving of his house; by which he condemned the world, and became heir of the righteousness which is by faith" (Hebrews 11:7). This is the standard by which Noah lived, the standard that caused him to live right before God in a wicked world around him.

First we're told that he was *warned by God*. God had warned Noah that judgment was coming. He told him that rain was going to fall upon the earth for 40 days and 40 nights. God has also clearly told *us* that judgment is coming. If we can't see the inevitable judgment that hangs upon the world right now, we're simply closing our eyes to what's going on around us. Even those who are not necessarily believers—the survivalists—can tell that hard times are coming, and so they are preparing themselves in their hideaway fortresses with their arsenals and freeze-dried foods. If we as the people of God cannot see the coming judgment, we need to pay more careful attention to signs around us.

God Gives His Warnings

The book of Daniel relates the story of King Belshazzar, who was mocking the Lord and thinking he could continually get away with his sin and disobedience to what God's Word said. One day as he was having a drunken party with his cohorts, the finger of God began to write on the wall. The message was to Belshazzar: "You have been weighed in the balances and found to be lacking" (Daniel 5:27). In other words, "God has weighed you in His balances, and you have been found to be a lightweight, Belshazzar! There's no substance to your life. You're all fluff." This man was warned, and so are we.

We have been warned by God, and we need to take action as a result of it. Noah was "moved with reverence" which means awe and reverence of God. To be reverent toward God simply means that we understand His greatness, His sovereignty, and His holiness. It means that we don't question Him at every turn and always want to understand everything He does, but just trust God to know what He is doing. This is not blind faith; it is *realistic* faith. It is simply acknowledging that God knows what He is doing and that we should obey Him.

The best way for us to come into an attitude of reverence with the Lord is to spend time in His presence. If we spend time in the presence of God, we will learn how great He is and how much we need Him, and we will come into a natural place of reverence. This reverence will cause us to want to obey God, because reverence begets obedience. The reason that many people are not obedient to God is because they are not reverent, and the reason they are not reverent is because they are not spending time with the Lord.

Reverence Produces Action

Not only was Noah walking with God and being warned of God, but, as he was moved with reverence, *he did something about it: He prepared an ark.* His reverence for the Lord produced action. Scripture tells us that he did according to all that the Lord commanded him. If Noah had not prepared an ark in obedience to God, would he have perished? The answer is yes! God had given him a warning, and there were certain things that Noah needed to do as a result of that warning.

Yet it was not Noah's efforts that saved him, because the ark that he built had no mast or sail. It was really God that guided him. So God is not telling us that our efforts save us, but He is telling us that if we are saved we should show some action as a result of it. James 2:18 tells us, "Show me your [alleged] faith without works and I will show you my faith by my works." In other words, if we are really saved, we should *produce action.*

In Noah's life the action was the preparing of an ark. In your life it could be the preparing of your life, resulting in a life of obedience and service to the Lord. We are told that as Noah prepared the ark it was to the saving of his household. As we read about the life of Noah we find that he lived 120 years but never had a single convert except those in his own family. That could get downright discouraging! Yet Noah had his family come to know the Lord, and they joined him on the ark of deliverance.

The Number One Mission Field

I believe that a person's number one mission field is his or her own family. If you are a husband of a wife who doesn't know Christ, she is your number one mission field. If your children don't know the Lord (or perhaps your parents don't), that's where true evangelism should begin.

When Noah prepared the ark for the saving of his house, Scripture says that by doing this he *condemned the world*. This doesn't mean that Noah walked around pointing his finger at people who were not believers, condemning them for their lack of relationship with God. Rather, it means that because of Noah's reverence toward God, resulting in his uncompromising obedience, it became obvious that these people were living evil lives.

When you are living as light in Jesus Christ, you are a radical contrast to those who are not living for the Lord. And it can really hurt to be rejected by your friends. Perhaps they mock you or make fun of you. But remember that Jesus said, "Woe unto you when all men speak well of you" (Luke 6:26). It isn't necessarily a good sign when everyone approves of everything you do. If you're really serving the Lord, you'll be harassed at times. The Bible tells us that all who live godly in Christ Jesus shall suffer persecution (2 Timothy 3:12). It is the inevitable result of following the Lord.

Are you living an uncompromised life for Jesus Christ? Are you moving in reverence? Are you putting your faith into action? Are you being what a last-days believer should really be?

Waiting for the Day

Second Peter chapter 3 tells us that the day of the Lord will come as a thief in the night, and all the elements will melt in fervent heat. Since this world will be dissolved, we ought to live godly lives and be found of God *in peace, without spot, and blameless*.

Noah was waiting for the flood, but we're waiting for the fire. The day of the Lord is coming—the day in which He will judge this world. This should affect our lives, causing us to live differently from the world around us. The Bible tells us that we should be found of Him "in peace." This word "peace" literally means "a serene confidence, free from fears and agitating passions and moral conflicts." That's the attitude in which we should be living right now as a child of God—in a serene confidence that is free from fears, agitating passions, and moral conflicts within our old nature. We can be free from these things as we walk in the power of God's Holy Spirit.

Confidence As We Wait

When Paul wrote to the church of Thessalonica he was addressing a church that was living in the expectancy of the Lord's return. He encouraged these believers, "Be at peace among yourselves" (1 Thessalonians 5:13).

In another one of his letters Paul said, "For God has not given us the spirit of fear, but of power and of love, and of a sound mind" (2 Timothy 1:7). He's saying, "Don't be afraid; and if there are people who are afraid, comfort them and support them; don't condemn them but encourage them." Why? Because, as he wrote in 1 Thessalonians 5:9, the Lord has not appointed us to wrath but to obtain salvation through our Lord Jesus Christ. In other

words, God will not put us through that time of judgment reserved for the people who have not followed
Him: "The Lord knows how to deliver the godly out
of temptations and to reserve the unjust unto the
day of judgment to be punished" (2 Peter 2:9). He
knows how to deliver those who are serving Him.

Looking at the life of Noah, God delivered him
first, and then the judgment came. It was not until
Noah was safely within the ark that the judgment
came upon the world. So don't be walking in fear.
Instead, be like Noah, living as a last-days believer,
moving with reverence and putting your faith into
action as you walk with God and await Christ's coming!

Chapter 3

3
Ready Till He Comes

In the book of Revelation God describes two primary churches that would exist in the last days. If you are a Christian you *are* a member of one of these two churches. These churches are not listed as Presbyterian, Methodist, Baptist, etc., but are listed as the church of Laodicea and the church of Philadelphia—the church of *lukewarmness* and the church of *revival*.

The question you must now ask yourself is: Which one of these churches am I a part of? Before you immediately decide that you're in the revival church, first read the "litmus test" on your present spiritual condition. In the book of Revelation (which is a last-days scenario that God revealed to the Apostle John on the Island of Patmos), John was caught up in a "spiritual time machine" and shown future events as they would happen. John then recorded these future events exactly as they were revealed to him. Just prior to Christ's graphic description of the deliverance of the church and the Great Tribulation following, He revealed to John the stages of church history and the condition of the churches before His return to earth.

The Church At the End

In Revelation 3:15-17 God says to the Laodicean church, "I know thy works, that thou art neither cold nor hot . . . So then because thou art lukewarm, and neither cold nor hot, I will spue thee out of my mouth. Because thou sayest, 'I am rich, and increased with goods, and have need of nothing,' and knowest not that thou art wretched, and miserable, and poor, and blind, and naked."

This Laodicean-type church (the lukewarm church or person) has the attitude that they really don't need anything. These are the people who, when they read the Bible, they think they know it all already. When they hear something about the Lord they feel they already have all the knowledge that they need. In other words, they're quite content in the state they're in.

I believe that this is one of the greatest dangers for a Christian—this condition in which we are totally content with our spiritual growth and see no need for change. But the fact is that when we stop changing we stop growing. We must constantly be pressing on toward the mark of the prize of the high calling of God in Christ Jesus. It is wrong to think that we have already come to the full maturity available to a Christian. Even the Apostle Paul, after years of serving the Lord, said, "It's not like I already attained or am already perfect, but I'm following after that for which I am apprehended." In other words, "I've got a lot of growing to do, and I haven't quite made it yet."

Some people believe they've reached a state of spiritual perfection and no longer sin in this life. A man once came up to C.H. Spurgeon at a Christian retreat and said that he had reached a state of spiritual perfection. Spurgeon picked up a pitcher of ice-cold water and poured it on the man's head. When the man became angry and reacted like any normal person would if cold water were poured on his head, Spurgeon said, "Well, now I know what spiritual perfection you've come to!" We're living in a facade if we think we have all we need; we must constantly see our need for growth.

Cooled Down?

The lukewarm person doesn't think he needs to grow or change; he's satisfied with his present condition. He is not usually a cold person gone warm but a hot person gone cool. In other words, the lukewarm person is a believer who has gone backwards in his Christian experience. It probably started when he began to abandon his first love or got himself out of the place where he could really be loving God and where God could actively bless him.

There is a difference between carnality and lukewarmness. Carnality is an arrested state of spiritual development. It's a condition in which a person is struggling with his old nature and is trying to serve the Lord, but he just can't quite make it. This is the dilemma that Paul wrote about in Romans chapter 7: "The good that I want to do, I don't do, and the bad things I don't want to do I end up doing."

But the lukewarm person is no longer struggling with sin; he has given up and is now defeated. Another difference between carnality and lukewarmness is that the lukewarm person is satisfied with himself and is therefore immune to the truth.

Why would these people be lukewarm? Revelation 3:17 says that they were increased with goods. In other words, they placed more emphasis on physical things than on spiritual things. There's nothing wrong with having possessions as a Christian; it only becomes wrong when the possessions have you. Jesus said, "Where your treasure is, there will your heart be also" (Matthew 6:21). If your heart is set on material possessions and on getting more, then you can be a candidate for lukewarmness.

The Lukewarm Facade

Jesus said that if we really want to be His disciples, we must have the proper perspective about material possessions. In Luke 14:33 He said, "If any man come after me and forsake not all that He has [or surrender claim to and say goodbye to] he cannot be my disciple." We must take all that we have, "our" life, "our" spouse, "our" possessions, etc. and say, "Lord, they belong to You. I dedicate them to You, and whatever You want to use I make available to You." The lukewarm person thinks that because he has all his physical needs met, he doesn't need to be spiritual. But he is deceived in this, because the Bible says that he is spiritually poor, miserable, wretched, blind, and naked.

It's something like the children's story of the emperor's new clothes. The emperor's tailor was told that he had to have a garment ready, but since he couldn't get it ready in time, he realized that he had to do some quick thinking. When the emperor came to the tailor asking for his garment, the tailor nervously responded, "I have it right here, sire," and quickly made up a lie as he held up his hands as though he were holding a garment. He then told the emperor, "This is the garment that I have prepared for you, and all those who are walking in truth will see it." The emperor, rather than admit he was not walking in truth, went along with the lie, pretending that he too saw it. So the tailor picked up the imaginary garment and draped it over the emperor's shoulders. The emperor then walked out of the tailor's room thinking that he was clothed in the most beautiful garment of all time, when in reality he was naked.

As he walked down the street in his great processional and all of the people bowed down, none would dare say to the emperor, "You have no clothes on." Many blushed, and some giggled, but none dared speak the truth. Finally a little child turned to his mother and said, "Mommy, why isn't the emperor wearing any clothes?" Then the emperor realized that his facade was over.

This is like the lukewarm person walking about in his self-righteous attitude, not realizing that he needs spiritual help.

Never Quite Enough

But God provides a solution to the lukewarm dilemma. He says, "I counsel thee to buy of me gold tried in the fire, that thou mayest be rich, and white raiment, that thou mayest be clothed, and that the shame of thy nakedness do not appear; and anoint thine eyes with eyesalve, that thou mayest see" (Revelation 3:18). God is telling this person that he needs to buy spiritual wealth. He needs to get back to spiritual things and put God's concerns first. He needs to "seek first the kingdom of God and His righteousness," and not seek first his own temporal needs.

This is really what Jesus was speaking of when He said, "Lay up for yourselves treasures in heaven, where neither moth nor rust doth corrupt, and where thieves do not break through nor steal; for where your treasure is, there will your heart be also" (Matthew 6:20,21). Everything we do on this earth for the kingdom of God translates into spiritual treasure that we will have waiting for us long after these temporal things on earth are gone.

Many believers can never get quite enough possessions, though they are continually accumulating more and more. It's sort of like leading the donkey with the carrot dangling in front of his face—always moving toward it but never quite getting there. Some people are no wiser than the donkey.

It starts when we're children. We always want a toy that's a little better, a little more sophisticated. Some people never outgrow this behavior. As the saying puts it, "The only difference between men and boys is the price of their toys."

A husband might say to his wife, "Honey, I've just got to get this new turntable for my stereo system. It's the latest laser digital turntable. It even turns the records over." So he buys his new turntable and then comes back to his wife and says, "Dear, now that I have this new laser digital turntable, I need these speakers so I can get the sound quality out of the turntable. The speakers are rather large, about 30 feet high, but the sound will be incredible." So he gets a second mortgage on his house to buy the speakers, then retruns one more time to his wife: "Honey there's one other thing left. Now that I have this new digital laser turntable and these 30-foot high speakers, I need a new amplifier to power them because my old one can't quite do it. At the stereo store they have this nuclear-powered amplifier. There is some occasional radioactive leakage, but the sound is incredible!" And on and on he goes.

If you can be satisfied with what you have, you have truly learned a great lesson. Paul said, "Having food and clothes let us be content, for godliness with contentment is great gain" (1 Timothy 6:6).

Change Your Direction

In addition to putting spiritual things first, we need to simply repent. God says in Revelation 3:19, "As many as I love, I rebuke and chasten; be zealous therefore, and repent." The wording that He uses here for love is very beautiful; He says, "As many as I *dearly and tenderly love* I rebuke and chasten."

Perhaps as you're reading this you may be a lukewarm person sensing the chastening of the Lord. Perhaps God is speaking to your heart and bringing to your attention the fact that you need to come out of this dilemma. God is not pointing a finger of condemnation toward you, but is holding out a hand of compassion toward you. As you look at that hand, remember that it was pierced for you. That's how much God loves you. He wants you to change your direction and return to close fellowship with the Lord Jesus Christ.

In Revelation 3:20 Jesus says to the lukewarm person, "Behold, I stand at the door and knock; if any man hear my voice and open the door, I will come in to him, and sup with him, and he with me." This verse is often used to speak to unbelievers to tell them that they need to invite Christ into their lives (and it does apply to this very well), but the verse is directed primarily to the lukewarm person who has drifted into a state of spiritual apathy. God is saying to that person, "Open the door and I will come in and sup with you."

Sharing in Love

We have to understand what the word "sup" really means in order to appreciate the meaning of this verse. In the Middle East culture when people "sup" together it is not a formal kind of meal. They don't sit at a table with linen napkins on their laps and beautiful silverware in their hands and worry about which hand they hold the knife in. Instead, they recline around a very low table. Rather than having his own individual plate, each person is given a piece of bread, which he dips into different sauces and foods. The meal is a sort of community sharing. It's a casual time when people enter into great fellowship with one another. Many times these meals take hours to eat.

This is the kind of relationship that God wants to have with you—not a formal sitting at a fancy table with you saying, "Lord, will You please pass the salt?" Not a fast-food, drive-through, quick-blessing relationship, either, but rather a casual, close, lengthy, intimate fellowship, in which you share in a love relationship with Jesus Christ.

Late for the Wedding

As a last-days believer (which I hope you are), there is not time for lukewarmness, for Jesus is returning soon, and we must be ready. Many times when speaking on His soon coming Jesus would warn of the need to be watching and ready. The parable of the ten virgins is a classic illustration of this. Jesus, speaking to the people, used the illustration of the Middle Eastern wedding, with the people symbolized by the virgins or bride and Himself as the Bridegroom.

He said, "Then shall the kingdom of heaven be likened unto ten virgins, which took their lamps and went forth to meet the bridegroom. And five of them were wise, and five were foolish. They that were foolish took their lamps, and took no oil with them, but the wise took oil in their vessels with their lamps.

While the bridegroom tarried, they all slumbered and slept. And at midnight there was a cry made, 'Behold, the bridegroom cometh! go out to meet him!' Then all those virgins arose and trimmed their lamps. And the foolish said unto the wise, 'Give us of your oil, for our lamps are gone out.' But the wise answered, 'Not so, lest there be not enough for us and you; but go rather to them that sell, and buy for yourselves.' And while they went to buy, the bridegroom came; and they that were ready went in with him to the marriage; and the door was shut. Afterward came also the other virgins, saying, 'Lord, Lord, open to us!' But he answered and said, 'Verily I say unto you, I know you not.' Watch therefore, for ye know neither the day nor the hour wherein the Son of man cometh" (Matthew 25:1-13).

Some of us might have a hard time understanding this, since our weddings aren't usually conducted like this. In that culture a wedding could last several days; the guests were invited and simply told to wait for the bridegroom to make his appearance. The bridegroom could arrive at any hour, morning or evening. When the call was given, "Behold the bridegroom is coming—go to meet him," if you were not ready you would miss the ceremony.

We are told that ten virgins were waiting. Five were believers and five were not. It is interesting to notice that the five who were not believers were still called virgins and had lamps. So they looked like authentic believers from the outside but lacked a real relationship with God.

Imitation Believers

This comes back to the lukewarm person. You may be religious, live morally, and even attend church regularly, yet not be a Christian! Going to church doesn't make you a Christian any more than driving through a McDonald's makes you a Big Mac!

The Bible describes these imitation believers as people who "have a form of godliness but deny the power thereof." Even though these religious people call Jesus Lord, and ask Him to open the door to the wedding after His arrival, He says, "I know you not." Jesus mentioned at another time the same situation in which these same type of people would say, "Lord, did we not prophesy in Your name? Did we not cast out demons in Your name? Did we not in Your name do many wonderful works?" and He would reply to them, "Depart from me, you workers of iniquity. I never knew you!" God forbid that this would apply to anyone reading this book. Yet if you trust in anything or anyone besides Jesus Christ for your salvation, you're on shaky ground.

Chapter
4

4
Sharing Till He Comes

There is another facet of the last-days church that Jesus describes in the book of Revelation. This is the church that is in the midst of revival. This is the person who is fervently serving the Lord. Perhaps you don't find yourself fitting in the lukewarm church. This one might fit you better.

Revelation 3:8,10 tells us, "I know thy works: behold, I have set before thee an open door, and no man can shut it: for thou hast a little strength, and hast kept my word, and hast not denied my name . . . Because thou hast kept the word of my patience, I also will keep thee from the hour of temptation, which shall come upon all the world, to try them that dwell upon the earth."

This is not a super-powered church. It is a mistake to think that Jesus cannot return until the church is in a super-powered state, until the church has perfected and cleansed itself. The church will indeed be perfected, but not by itself; it is *God* who will do the perfecting (Ephesians 5:25-27). Thinking that the church has to be perfect before the Lord comes back makes about as much sense as taking a load of dirty laundry, throwing it on the ground, and ordering it to wash itself and dry itself and fold itself! The church is *incapable* of cleaning itself. *God* is going to do the scrubbing. He is going to do the presenting. *He* is going to take all the necessary precautions to prepare us for His coming. If Jesus could not come back until the church were perfect on earth, Jesus could never come back at all!

The church of Philadelphia is not a superchurch, but rather a church that has a little strength. The word for strength here means "like a person coming back to live." That is really the situation with the church of Philadelphia. It's a revival, meaning that God has revived something that once was. Looking back over church history during hundreds of years, we find that the church has at times sunk to an incredible low. Some of the most abominable things in history have been done in the name of Christianity. But the last-days church of Philadelphia has a little strength; it is a church coming back to life.

The Open Door

What does God say to us who are living in this last-days church? First He says that He has set before us an open door that no man can shut. And there is indeed an open door set before us that is unprecedented in world history—a door to preach the gospel to many people who have never heard it before. God has opened a door for you. It may be in your household, reaching your unsaved husband or raising your children in the way of the Lord. It may be a door in your neighborhood, reaching the neighbors that have not yet come to know Christ. It may be a door in your community, reaching out to those people in your community who do not know the Lord. Or it may be a door into farther places. You never know what plan God has in store for you.

Not long ago I had an opportunity to visit a land with the largest population of any country in the world—the land of China, with almost a billion people. To see so many people who did not know Jesus Christ truly moved my heart. I thank God that He is providing a great outpouring of His Holy Spirit in China, so that thousands and thousands of Chinese people are coming to the Lord right now in the greatest revival in Chinese history. We've gotten word that entire communities in China are coming to know the Lord.

The Photographic Gospel

Before our trip to China I had heard that there was an incredible fascination among the Chinese people over "instant" photography and Polaroid-type cameras. I had heard that if you took a photograph of one of the people, a great crowd would come around to watch it develop. I thought to myself, "What if I were to take some pictures of the people and give them to the people as a gift with a little bonus on the back of the photo—a Scripture about God's love for them?" So I took John 3:16 ("For God so loved the world that He gave His only begotten Son, that whosoever believeth in Him should not perish but have everlasting life") in Chinese and had a couple of hundred stickers made up.

Then my wife and I (along with some other believers) left for China. I could hardly wait to try this out, so we went to the main square in Peking and began to photograph the people. They were very friendly and excited and began to gather in giant crowds around us to watch this miracle of the photo developing before their eyes. Then we took out the John 3:16 stickers in Chinese and stuck them to the back of the photos and gave them to the people. They loved it!

What's God?

One warm summer evening in Peking we walked outside our hotel and watched hundreds of Chinese ride by on their bicycles. Pretty soon a crowd gathered around us, and we tried to communicate with them to no avail, when one of them began to speak English. He told us he was a student at the university there, and we began to talk with him. I told him that God loved him, to which he replied, "What's God?" I couldn't believe he didn't even know that God existed.

We shared more with this young man about how God demonstrated His love for him by sending His Son to die for him. Another couple we were with also shared with him, as well as with some of the other students who spoke English, and by the next night they had led four of the students to the Lord! What a privilege! This was one of the doors that God opened for us, but we might have missed it had we not made ourselves available to Him that evening.

China is a door that has opened only recently and may close again soon. Perhaps God would call you to walk through it.

The Door Is Where You Are

There is a door open, but it won't be open forever. Time is short, and we must make proper use of the opportunities set before us. We need to have our eyes opened to see that the harvest is plenteous but the laborers few. The population of our country alone is well over 200 million. Even with the blitz of television and radio evangelism and publication, there are still many people who have not had Christ shared with them on a one-to-one basis.

God can use you to do that. He has set before you an open door. God wants to give us spiritual bifocal lenses, so that we don't see just what's close to us, but also what's far away from us. Even if we do not personally go to these areas, at least we can support in prayer and giving those who do go.

Sometimes we think of what it would be like to travel the world sharing Christ full-time, and how exciting that would be. You may be a housewife reading this book and thinking you're not important, but you have literally dozens of opportunities to share God's love with people every day! Your neighbors need the Lord. Have you told them about Jesus? The kids on your block need Jesus. Have you told them? One lady in our fellowship started a weekly Bible study for all the kids on her block, and God began a little revival right in her neighborhood.

That checker down at the market needs to know about Jesus. Have you told him or her?

Many times God puts us into one of His "divine setups." It's probably happened to you. You're standing in line to pay for your groceries, flipping through some magazine, when someone says, "Look at the price of this food! What is this world coming to?" Another person says, "Well, with all this talk of the threat of nuclear war, it doesn't even matter—trying to ignore them and to just read your magazine. But your heart is beating so loudly that you're afraid someone will hear it. You hear the gentle but firm voice of the Holy Spirit speaking to your heart and saying "Tell them." Then one of the people says, "You'd almost think God wasn't paying any attention. I wonder if *He* has anything to say about this."

Finally you speak. Perhaps your voice quivers a little, but you know a divine set-up when you see one. I think the hardest thing about sharing Jesus is the first few words that come out of your mouth. You may be worried that you won't have enough to say, but it's really like shaking up a bottle of soda. Once you open it, it's hard to stop it.

Perhaps you're a businessman, or a secretary, or a factory worker, or a student. Those people around you need Jesus. Tell them! There is an open door before you. Go through it before it closes.

True Spiritual Grit

Christ tells us in Revelation 3:10 that those who keep the word of His patience will be kept from the hour of temptation, the Great Tribulation Period. The word "patience" here is based on a Greek word meaning "steadfast endurance" or simply "persevering." This is kind of like a "spiritual true grit" that God wants His people to have.

The Apostle James tells us that the way we get this kind of perseverance is through trials and the testing of our faith. He tells us that the trying of our faith works perseverance, and that we should let perseverance have its perfect work so that we may be perfect and fully developed spiritually (James 1:3,4).

One thing we really need as Christians is some good old persevering endurance. Too many Christians are spiritual cream puffs who give up when God takes them through His spiritual boot camp. They want the easy life. They want everything given to them on a silver platter. But following Jesus Christ is a life of sacrifice. It's a life of persevering during times of hardship, trial, and affliction, regardless of our emotions.

When Jesus told the parable of the sower, He talked about the four different kinds of seeds that fell on different kinds of ground. The only seeds that really broke ground and brought forth fruit were those that fell on the good ground. These represented believers with an honest and good heart who heard the Word of God and brought forth fruit with perseverance (Luke 8:5-15). The reason those seeds lasted was because they hung in there. They applied themselves. This is the key to running the spiritual race set before us.

Releasing God's Power

God is not asking you to use will power to live the Christian life. Rather, He's telling you that you must persevere even when times are hard, even if your family and friends forsake you. You must persevere even if you don't feel like it. The Lord will give you all the power you need if you ask Him for it. It's a little like getting water from a faucet: You don't just hold your glass under the faucet and wait. You turn the handle, and then the water comes. You must release, or appropriate, the water you need.

God's power for you is available. You must by faith receive the power that is available from the Holy Spirit. Simply ask God to fill you with all the power He has for you, then receive it by believing His Word.

Sometimes when the Lord brings us to the beginning of a spiritual valley and begins to lead us through it, we protest, "No, Lord! Please, let's go *around* this valley." He might answer, "This will strengthen you, and give you that perseverance you need to live for Me. True spiritual fruit doesn't grow on those spiritual mountaintop experiences, but rather down here in the valleys." "But Lord . . . I'm afraid." Jesus might respond, "Don't worry. I'll be with you. I will never leave you nor forsake you. You must come through these valleys to get to the next mountaintop." You think about that for a couple of moments and say, "How about if You just airlift me to the next mountaintop!" He then takes you by the hand and leads you into the valley.

There are times when the Lord allows our faith to be tried and we cannot consciously "feel" His presence. He is asking us at that point to walk by faith in what His Word says, and not by our feelings. It is vital during these times that we do not give up and throw in the towel, but rather keep on moving.

Keep Moving with Christ

David wrote in Psalm 23, "Yea, though I walk through the valley of the shadow of death, I will fear no evil, for Thou art with me: Thy rod and Thy staff, they comfort me." David did not say, "Yea, though I *sit* in the valley or collapse and give up in the valley," but, "yea, though I *walk* through the valley."

The key to developing this spiritual perseverance is found in Hebrews 12:1,2: "Let us lay aside every weight, and the sin which so easily besets us, and let us run with *perseverance* the race that is set before us, looking unto Jesus, the Author and Finisher of our faith, who, for the joy that was set before Him, endured the cross, despising the shame, and is set down at the right hand of the throne of God."

Here we have the key, the incentive, the motive for coming through our valleys and trials: looking unto Jesus! This means that we keep our eyes set on Him no matter what we're going through. We live to please Him, so that we can look into His eyes one day and hear Him say to us, "Well done, you good and faithful servant. Enter into the joy of your Lord!"

Watching and Walking

One day Simon Peter saw Jesus walking on the Sea of Galilee and called out to Him, "Lord, if it's You, tell me to come!" So Jesus told him to come, and Peter climbed off the boat, never taking his eyes off Jesus. He put one foot on the water, but, rather than sinking, he actually stood on it! He then carefully put his other foot out, and it too did not sink, but stayed on top of the water. As Peter kept looking at Jesus he stepped closer and closer and was doing the miraculous.

Perhaps Peter thought to himself, "I hope James and John can see me now!" Maybe he even looked over his shoulder to see if they were watching. Or it could have been that Peter said, "Wait a second, I can't do this—this is impossible!" We don't know exactly what happened, but whatever it was, Peter began to sink under the water. Then he cried out, "Lord, save me!" to which Jesus reached out to him and said, "O you of little faith, why did you doubt?"

One thing is certain: As long as Peter had his eyes on Jesus he could do the impossible, but as soon as he took his eyes off Jesus, he began to sink. The same is true of us: We can come through any circumstance, any valley, if we keep our eyes on Jesus.

Corrie ten Boom, who survived the terrors of a Nazi concentration camp during World War Two, gave an insight to what kept her going. She wrote, "Look around and be distressed, look within and be depressed, look at Jesus and be at rest." Keeping our eyes on Jesus will give us the perseverance we need as we follow the Lord in these last days.

Jesus Kept Going

Hebrews 12:2 also tells us that it was for the joy set before Him that Jesus endured the cross. Can you imagine the spiritual valley that Jesus went through after having His back ripped open by the Roman scourging, His beard pulled from His face, the crown of thorns smashed into His head, and then being compelled to bear His own cross through the streets of Jerusalem? Yet something kept Him going. It certainly wasn't any thought of His own personal gain, because it was a total sacrifice on His part. Some wept for Him that day, but many others cursed Him and mocked Him. Yet He went through with it. Coming to the Place of the Skull (Golgotha), He was crucified. There he bore all the corruption, the ungodliness, the sin of the world upon Himself.

What was His motive? What kept Him going? *You!* The joy set before Him was the knowledge that through His suffering and agony *you and I* could have a relationship with Him. He went through the ultimate valley for you and me. Can't we go through a small valley for Him? He endured the worst suffering for us. Can't we endure comparatively a little suffering for Him?

He died for you. Will you live for Him?

Keeping the Word

Another thing that we as Christians need to be doing in these last days is to *keep God's Word*. This does not mean to just have a collection of Bibles on a shelf gathering dust, nor does it mean to have a Bible well-marked with notes, for it is not how you mark your Bible, but how your Bible marks you! Keeping the Word of God means that we stay in the Word of God, that we hold it near to our hearts and apply it to our day-to-day living.

Paul wrote to Timothy, "Preach the Word; be instant in season, out of season . . . For the time will come when they will not endure sound doctrine, but after their own lusts they will heap to themselves teachers, having itching ears; and they shall turn away their ears from the truth and be turned unto fables. But watch thou in all things [and] endure afflictions" (2 Timothy 4:2-5).

There are going to be people who will not keep God's Word in these last days. Many people would much rather hear a message that tickles their ears. For example, people love to hear messages about financial prosperity. They love to hear messages about all the good things that *God can give them,* but they don't always like to hear messages about repentance or sacrifice or what they can *give to God.*

I believe that if Christian books, teaching cassettes, and television and radio ministeries are doing what they are supposed to, they will stimulate our hunger for personal study of the Bible. No amount of reading commentaries or Christian books will replace our need for a regular diet of the Word of God. At best these other things should be appetizers to stimulate our hunger for the main course, the Word of God.

I hope this book will cause you to search the Scriptures and not just believe the things that I state here, but to check them according to the Word. The combination of regular study of the Scriptures and putting them into action along with the power of God's Holy Spirit is what we need for a proper balance spiritually. "Too much Word and we *dry up;* too much Spirit and we *blow up;* enough of both and we *grow up*."

Crucial Nutrition

It is truly amazing how many believers neglect a regular, daily study of the Scriptures. Then they find themselves weak spiritually but can't understand why. I read a statement that said, "Seven days without reading the Bible makes one *weak*." You wouldn't think about skipping meals for a week, yet the Word of God doesn't seem to have the same value to us as a meal. Job had the right perspective when he wrote, "I have esteemed the words of His mouth more than my necessary food!" (Job 23:12).

We need to follow the example of the man who is blessed by God: "His delight is in the law of the Lord, and in His law doth he meditate day and night" (Psalm 1:2). This key word "meditate" means to ponder and contemplate. We not only need to *read* the Word but we also need to *feed* on it, pondering and contemplating as we read.

We can't read the Scriptures as though we were eating from a fast-food restaurant. Rather, we should slowly ponder the Word and allow the Spirit of God to speak to us as though we were eating in a very expensive restaurant. Sometimes when my wife and I go out to a nice restaurant and I gulp down my food like I'm at Burger King, she reminds me that the steak I'm gulping down is costing me $1.25 a bite. Then I chew much more slowly. It is better for us to read just a few passages at a time and really contemplate their meaning than to read several chapters in a speed-reading approach and forget what we've read.

Chapter
5

5
Active Till He Comes

As we wait for Jesus to return, there are certain things that we need to be doing. There is a parable in Luke 19 concerning a master who went on a journey. Before he left he gave to each of his servants a talent (a measure of money) and said to them, "Occupy till I come." This phrase can also be translated, "Invest until I return."

When the master returned from his journey, he went to one of the men to whom he had given one of the talents, and the man said, "Master, your talent has gained ten talents." The master replied, "Well done, you good servant; you have been faithful in very little, so you will have authority over ten cities." The second man said, "Master, your talent has gained five talents." The master replied, "Well done, you good and faithful servant; I will make you ruler over five cities." Then he went on to a man who said, "I didn't harvest what you gave me—I buried it in the ground." The master reproved him because he did not use what he had.

This parable teaches us that, as we wait for the Lord to return, we should wisely invest what He has put in our care—that is, our lives.

Redeeming the Time

Paul exhorts us in Ephesians 5:16 to "redeem the time, because the days are evil." The word "redeem" actually means "to make wise and sacred use of every opportunity." We must realize that all we have is really on loan from the Lord. So often we say, "my house," "my car," "my wife and children," "my money," or "my future," but the fact of the matter is that if we are Christians they are not ours at all but God's. Our very existence is a gift from the Lord. The very breath that you are drawing as you read this book is really a gift from God.

The Bible teaches us that God has bought us with a price; when Jesus Christ died on the cross for our sins, He paid the penalty for the sins we have committed, and now we belong to Him. God gave us His best, and now He wants us to give Him our best.

A farmer had a cow which gave birth to twin calves. The farmer told his wife, "The Lord blessed us with two calves, so to show my thanks I'm going to give one of the calves to the Lord!" His wife responded, "Which calf are you giving to the Lord?" The farmer said, "I haven't decided yet." Later on one of the calves grew sick and died. At that point the farmer came to his wife and said, "I have sad news—the Lord's calf just died." So often, rather than giving God our best, we give Him our leftovers!

The Necessary Change

This must change if we are to be pleasing to the Lord as we await His return. He is asking us to take our lives and wisely invest them and use them as we anticipate His coming and His return to the earth. Paul continues in his statement in Ephesians by writing that one way to make wise and sacred use of every opportunity is to know what the will of God is for our lives (5:17).

Can you imagine your response if Jesus said He was coming to dinner at your house, as He said to Zacchaeus in the sycamore tree? Realizing that the Almighty God, the Creator of the universe, was going to dine with you, what do you think you would serve Him? A TV dinner? Last night's leftover meatloaf? Of course not! You would serve Him the best food you could buy, arranged on the finest china.

Yet when it comes to our personal lives and our time with the Lord, we often give Him our leftovers. Our time of prayer with Him is often the last thing we do in the evening. After we have read the paper and watched television, we give our last moments to Jesus as we drift off to sleep. When it comes to serving Him, we make ourselves available only as it is convenient to us—and let not God dare to suggest that we rearrange our schedule to do something for Him.

Yet when we're in need we never hesitate to storm the throne of God with our needs and constantly remind Him of His promise to take care of us! God gave us His absolute best when He sent His only beloved, cherished Son. He gave us the One who was dearest to His Heart. God expects no less from us.

Wake Up and Invest!

How can we wisely invest our lives? How can we occupy until He comes? The Bible teaches a number of ways to do this. One of these is found in Romans 13:11: "Knowing the time, that now it is high time to awake out of sleep, for now is our salvation nearer than when we believed." One of the first things we need to do as we occupy till He comes is to awake out of sleep. The Bible tells us that before we know Jesus Christ we are in a sort of spiritual slumber, not really aware of what's going on in the realm of the Spirit. God wants us to awake out of this.

If anyone has ever aroused you out of a dead sleep (perhaps with a phone call in the middle of the night), you were probably not totally coherent. You felt a bit groggy and were not totally aware of what was being said. When we wake people out of a dead sleep they sometimes act as though they were not sleeping at all; they try to be totally normal, but usually their slurred speech or lapses into snoring give them away. This is the kind of condition from which we need to awake.

No Spiritual False Alarm

Once while I was resting overnight on the eighteenth floor of a hotel the fire alarm went off. The man I was rooming with woke me up quickly, telling me that we had to get out of the hotel right away. My response was to tell him to go back to sleep, and to attempt to do the same myself. He finally brought me to my senses, and we got out of the hotel. (Fortuantely it was only a false alarm.) There are many believers today who think they have all the time in the world, so they keep putting off those things that God wants them to do with their lives. But the Lord keeps saying, "Wake up! My coming is near!"

The Bible says concerning the last days, "Let us not sleep, as do others, but let us watch and be sober. For they that sleep sleep in the night, and they that be drunken are drunken in the night. But let us who are of the day be sober, putting on the breastplate of faith and love, and for a helmet, the hope of salvation. For God hath not appointed us to wrath but to obtain salvation by our Lord Jesus Christ," (1 Thessalonians 5:6-9).

We Christians need to be moving onward in our relationship with the Lord. God wants to awaken us out of our passive, lazy, sterile Christian experience in which our relationship with God is boring and un-interesting. God wants us to awake to righteousness, to put on our spiritual armor, and to march and gain ground as we enter into the final days before Christ's return to the earth.

The Real Battle

In putting on this spiritual armor we have a battle to fight. It is a battle not fought with fists or swords or military might but rather with spiritual weapons. The battle is between the forces of darkness and the forces of light, and you are on the battlefield.

A young man came up to me one evening while I was walking with my wife and wanted me to read his newspaper propagating Communism. I listened to him talk for a couple of moments about what he believed, and when he was done I looked at him and said, "the real battle is much deeper than capitalism versus Communism or one cause against another. The real battle is the unseen one in the spiritual realm, and we will not see true peace on this earth until Jesus Christ returns to the earth."

Win or Lose?

The question is not whether we are going to engage in this spiritual battle, because we really have no choice. The question is whether we are going to be *victorious*. We are either going to win or lose, and the choice is up to us. Many believers are content to find some comfortable little foxhole and climb into it, putting their shield over them with their sword sticking out, in hopes that the enemy will fall on it and be killed.

Others are running in retreat and are even falling away from the Lord in these last days. We must not allow ourselves to retreat. Winston Churchill said, when London was being bombed during World War Two, that victory is not won by evacuation. We must not evacuate or even be content with holding our ground. We must attack and gain new ground spiritually as we put on the armor of light as spiritual soldiers of the Lord.

Jesus said that the gates of hell would not prevail against His church. He did not mean that as we just sit around complacently the forces of hell would not overtake us. What He meant was that as we aggressively move out spiritually, the gates of hell cannot stop us.

Remember the story of the shepherd boy David. When no one in the army of Israel had the courage to withstand the nine-foot Philistine enemy, Goliath, David recognized that this was not a battle between the Israelites and the Philistines but rather between good and evil. With this understanding David attacked his adversary! He didn't run from him or just hold his ground, but he attacked, saying to Goliath, "You come to me with a sword and spear and a shield, but I come to you in the name of the Lord of Hosts, the God of the armies of Israel, whom you have defied!" (1 Samuel 17:45). With this spiritual surge of courage he defeated his adversary with a well-placed stone. This is the way we as believers are to fight this spiritual battle—to attack!

Imitating Christ

Romans 13:13,14 tells us the same thing when it says, "Let us behave properly, as in the day, not in carousing and drunkenness, not in sexual promiscuity and sensuality, not in strife and jealousy. But put on the Lord Jesus Christ, and make no provision for the flesh in regard to its lusts" (NASB). To put on the Lord Jesus Christ means literally to enter into His views and interests, to be holy in His sight, and to imitate Him in all things.

They say that imitation is the sincerest form of flattery. To effectively imitate someone, you need to spend time with him to observe him. If you spend a lot of time with Jesus, you will naturally pick up those things of His nature. That is the thought Paul is conveying when he tells us to "put on the Lord Jesus Christ."

No Longer in Love?

Paul also says that we should "make no provision for the flesh." Sometimes we tell God we are sorry for our sins when deep down in the secret places of our heart we are already plotting when we will do them again. We need to avoid making any provision for our flesh. This is all part of putting on the Lord Jesus Christ.

A man can lose the spark of love that brought him and his wife together in the first place. He can lose that original closeness and intimacy, and fall into a marriage that is more like a legal partnership than a love relationship. In the same way we as Christians can enter into a legal relationship with God in which we are no longer in love with Him. When we're really in love with someone, all we can do is think about how we can please that person and how we can do things that will make that person happy. When we first meet Jesus Christ, that's how we are. We want to please Him. We want to make Him happy. We want to do things for Him. But as time goes on we can drift into an apathetic state.

If that has happened to you, and you have lost that spark that you had when you first were following Christ, then it's time to turn back to that first-love relationship and to renew your commitment to Him. That is the very foundation of your entire Christian life—loving Christ and drawing close to Him as you stay ready for His return to this earth.

God's primary purpose in creating us is that we might have an intimate love relationship with Him. Yet it is amazing how we can drift away from this into other things, even under the cloak of "spiritual activity." Did you know that it is possible to be active for God in every sense of the word—in Bible reading, in church attendance, in praying, etc.—and still get away from a close relationship of love with Jesus? God is more interested in our *inspiration* than our *perspiration*. Does this mean that God doesn't want us to be spiritually active and doing things for Him? Actually, it means the opposite: God wants us to be active in His service, but with the right motives.

Knowing Him

In 1 Chronicles 28:9 David gave a final charge to his son Solomon in which he gave a really wonderful standard for a believer to live by: "And thou, Solomon my son, know thou the God of thy father, and serve Him with a perfect heart and with a willing mind, for the Lord searcheth all hearts and understandeth all the imaginations of the thoughts; if thou seek Him, He will be found of thee, but if thou forsake Him, He will cast thee off forever." The perfect heart and willing mind stem from the foundation of *knowing God*. The word translated "know Him" means in the Hebrew "have a personal knowledge of, be acquainted with, appreciate, heed, and cherish."

This was also the motto of the Apostle Paul. As he suffered incredible difficulties in his service to the Lord, he said, "My determined purpose is to know Him, to become more intimately and deeply acquainted with Him through the power of His resurrection and the fellowship of His suffering." Is this our purpose in life? Are we experiencing this intimate fellowship with the Lord that He desires for us?

Close to the Lord

After His resurrection Jesus had an interesting conversation with Simon Peter. Peter had been fishing all night but had caught nothing. As he sat there in his fishing boat on the Sea of Galilee with James and John, he heard a very familiar voice call from the shore, "Boys, do you have any food?" They replied that they didn't, to which this Person told them to cast their net on the other side of the boat. As they did so their net became so full of fish that they couldn't pull it all in the boat.

John suddenly realized that this same incident had occurred a few years earlier in one of their first encounters with Jesus. He realized at this moment that the Stranger on the shore was the resurrected Christ. So John exclaimed, "It's the Lord!"

To this Peter responded by leaping out of the boat into the water and frantically swimming for shore. Peter didn't want to miss this opportunity to be close to his Lord, after his miserable experience of denying the Lord as he warmed himself at the fire outside the court of Caiaphas while Jesus was being questioned. As Peter drew close to the shore and saw the face of Jesus in the fire's glow, perhaps he thought of the other fire where three separate times he had denied his Master. As Peter drew closer, perhaps he was expecting Jesus to be looking on him with scorn or an expression of "How could you have done that?"

What Kind of Love?

But in contrast to what Peter had anticipated, as he drew closer to Jesus, he saw a tender, compassionate expression of understanding on his Lord's face. Jesus had been preparing a meal for His weary disciples, and as they leisurely ate their meal in the intentionally slow pace of the Middle East, there was not much conversation. Peter, who really cared for the Lord, wanted to say something, perhaps apologize, when Jesus broke the silence and spoke to Peter.

Peter's heart was pounding as Jesus looked him in the eyes and said, "Peter, do you love me *more than these?*" Peter's mind darted back to the time when he had pledged to the Lord, "Though all these others deny you, I will never deny you!" To this Jesus had responded, "Before the rooster has crowed you will have denied me three times." Peter had learned the hard way not to speak of his love by contrasting himself to others.

Yet the very word for love that Jesus used was one of great demand. When Jesus asked Peter if he loved Him, the word He used for love was the Greek word *agape*. There is really not a word in the English language that effectively expresses this term. The word *agape* means "the absorption of every part of your being in one passion." It is a word that implies the highest form of devotion, causing one to sacrifice anything in this love.

Peter was not able to say yes to this difficult question. Rather, he responded, "Yes, Lord, I love you." The word that Peter used for love was a completely different one than Jesus used. Peter's word was *phileo,* which means "a personal affection as for a close friend."

Jesus is asking you the same thing right now: Do you love Him? It's not enough to just like Him as a close, personal friend or companion; do you *agape* Him? Is your love for Jesus the absorption of *every* part of your being? This is God's ideal for you. This is the foundation of your life as a believer—that you serve Him because you truly love Him.

How to Stay in Love

Jude, in his short book in the New Testament, gives us a step-by-step way in which we can keep ourselves in a love relationship with Jesus Christ. Speaking of the last days, he tells us in verse 18 that there would be mockers and scoffers in the last days who would walk after their own ungodly lusts. In 2 Peter 3:4 we find that these same scoffers would say, "Where is the promise of His coming? Since our fathers fell asleep all things continue as they were." Sometimes we hear from people today, "Do you really believe that Jesus is coming back at any moment? My grandmothers used to tell me that. That's an old wives' fable."

Jude goes on: "These are they who separate themselves, sensual, having not the Spirit" (v. 19). Then in contrast he says, "But ye, beloved, building up yourselves on your most holy faith, praying in the Holy Spirit, *keep yourselves in the love of God,* looking for the mercy of our Lord Jesus Christ unto eternal life" (vv. 20,21). This is what we need to be doing as we await the coming of the Lord— to keep ourselves in the love of God.

Praying in the Spirit

But how do we do this? First of all, Jude says, "Build yourself up in your most holy faith, praying in the Holy Spirit." We need to be praying in the power of God's Spirit as we wait for Christ's return to the earth. To pray in the Spirit does not mean to go into some trancelike state, but rather it means to pray according to the will of God and in the power that He has made available to us as believers. This gets back to knowing Him and all that goes with it, resulting in a renewed prayer life. Conversation is much more meaningful with someone we know and love. When we first meet someone, conversation can be very awkward and uncomfortable. Prayer is simply conversing with God, speaking to Him and listening to Him.

When we truly have a two-way channel open between us and God, we will not pray for self-indulgent things. Such self-indulgent prayer I like to term "Cadillac faith," in which we claim lavish gifts for ourselves in the name of the Lord. If we begin to pray according to the will of God and start seeking the things in our life that He really wants, then we will begin seeing a transformation into the very image of Jesus Christ. True fellowship with God performs this metamorphosis.

Jude tells us that we must build ourselves up in our most holy faith, praying in the Holy Spirit and keeping ourselves in the love of God. This does not mean that we keep ourselves in a place where God can love us, because no matter what we do, God will always love us. What this verse means is that we are to keep ourselves in a place where we are loving God. The danger is not that God will stop loving us; it is that we will stop loving Him. The danger is not that God will *leave us,* but that we will *leave Him.* Jesus told us, "As the Father has loved me, so have I loved you; continue ye in my love." In other words, we should stay in a place where God can bless us.

Close to Christ

The prodigal son decided one day to leave his father's care and go off and waste his inheritance on riotous living. He went out and spent all that he had. But he became disillusioned, and empty-handed, and he decided to return to his father and ask to become as one of the hired servants. What the prodigal son had done was to get out of the place where his father could bless him even though his father had always loved him. This is evidenced by the fact that, when the prodigal returned, his father ran out to greet him. The prodigal had turned his back on his father, and as long as he was out in the world disgracing his father's name he was out of the place where his father could actively bless him. So to keep in God's love simply means to stay close to Him, where He can bless us and speak with us and guide us.

Jude tells us yet another way to keep ourselves in the love of God. In verse 21 he says, ". . .looking for the mercy of our Lord Jesus Christ." As we realize that Jesus could come at any moment, we should be looking for His mercy. It's something that compels us; it's something that motivates us; it's something that stimulates us to service. It makes us want to be truly ready to meet Him.

Chapter
6

6
Abiding Till He Comes

As a last-days believer, one of the things we're told we should be doing is found in 1 John 2:28: "Now little children, abide in Him, that, when He shall appear, we may have confidence, and not be ashamed before Him at His coming." Sometimes when we read this verse we just skim by it without paying careful attention to this important last-day activity that we as believers should be doing. *We should be abiding in Christ as we await His coming.*

Bearing Fruit for Christ

The word "abide" literally means "a permanence of position, one's dwelling place, holding and maintaining unbroken fellowship with another person." Jesus spent a lot of time explaining what the abiding relationship with Him was all about. In John 15:4 He told us, "Abide in me, and I in you. As the branch cannot bear fruit of itself, except it abide in the vine, no more can ye, except ye abide in me." What he meant by this was that God expects us to bring forth spiritual fruit.

This is actually one of the primary reasons that God created us. Jesus said in John 15:16, "Ye have not chosen me, but I have chosen you, and ordained you, that ye should go and *bring forth fruit, and that your fruit should remain.*" That is really God's plan for our life. Everything else becomes secondary to the importance of abiding and bringing forth fruit. Our career, what we do with our life, where we live,—all of these become secondary to the primary reason that God created us. God wants us to be spiritually fruitful believers.

The Bible tells us what this fruit of the Spirit is. We are told in the book of Galatians that this fruit is love, joy, peace, longsuffering, gentleness, goodness, faith, meekness, and temperance (Galatians 5:22,23). This is what the Lord desires for us to have in our life—to love God and to bring forth spiritual fruit. Jesus said in John 15:1,2, "I am the true vine, and my Father is the husbandman. Every branch in me that beareth not fruit He taketh away; and every branch that beareth fruit, he purgeth it, that it may bring forth more fruit." The branch that is connected to the vine has one primary purpose—to receive the vine's life-giving nourishment that gives the branch the ability to bring forth fruit. We as Christians must be receiving Christ's life by constantly abiding in Him. Only then can we bring forth fruit as described in Galatians. This is the kind of fruit that brings true glory to our God.

Getting Pruned by God

Christ also said that if we are abiding in Him, He will purge us or prune us back so that our fruit will be large and lasting. I used to have a peach tree, and I looked forward to the time when the tree would bring forth fruit and I could enjoy it all summer long. I went out and watched it each day as it got closer and closer to the time for the peaches to be ready, but I noticed that they never got any larger than the size of ping-pong balls. I couldn't understand what was wrong. Then someone told me that I needed to prune the tree and take off certain fruit so that the other fruit would grow larger. In other words, the tree needed constant care to come to its total fruition.

The same is true with us. God needs to purge us or prune us back—to remove those things in our lives that are a hindrance to our spiritual growth. God will remove whatever hindrance in our life that stops us from bearing spiritual fruit. If we really want to do what He wants us to do, we will allow His Holy Spirit to come and prune us back so that we might bring forth much fruit.

Perhaps you can think of something the Holy Spirit has been showing you that doesn't belong in your life. It could be a certain direction you are going, or a sin you are committing, or even a relationship that should not be. Don't be afraid of the loving hand of God removing a hindrance to your spiritual growth, for He only takes away to give you something better in its place!

Abiding in Christ

The key to all of this fruit-bearing is abiding in Jesus Christ. In John 15:7 He gives us a wonderful promise if we do abide in Him: "If ye abide in me, and my words abide in you, ye shall ask what ye will and it shall be done unto you." Jesus is telling us that if we are abiding in Him, if we are maintaining a permanence of position and not uprooting and replanting ourselves over and over, whatever we ask of God will be given to us.

If the Lord were to come to you and say, "Whatever you want, I will give it to you," what would you ask for? A new car? More money? If so, this shows that you are not truly abiding in Jesus Christ. If you are truly abiding in Christ your answer would be something like this: "Whatever You want to give me, Lord, that's what I'll receive. I want You to be glorified and I want Your will to be done." That is the attitude of a person who is truly abiding in Christ. His prayer is not dominated with selfish motives of getting more and more, but with wanting to be conformed into the image of Christ and with caring about the needs of other people.

Deep Roots

Abiding is a permanence of position. Suppose we were to buy a little tree at a nursery, plant it in a corner of our yard, and then a couple of days later say, "I think this tree would look better on the other side of the yard." We uproot the tree, take it to the other side of the yard, and plant it there. Then we change our mind again and decide that it would look better in our front yard, so we uproot it again and plant it in our front yard. By the time we're done uprooting that little tree and planting it over and over again, it will be in shock. We'll have to call the plant ambulance to come and save it.

If we as Christians one day are serving the Lord and the next day rip up our roots and turn our back on Him, and then recommit ourselves and begin to serve Him for a time, then uproot ourselves and go away from Him again, we are going to be in spiritual shock.

Jesus is saying, "If you really want to bring forth lasting fruit, you've got to get your roots in deep." This is not a flash-in-the-pan kind of experience. Sometimes people talk about a relationship with God as though it were a new toothpaste. They might say, "Try God and He will take all your troubles away." God is not a product that we take and then discard. He is the living Creator who made you and me, and He asks us not to just use Him when it's convenient but to submit to Him and serve Him with our whole heart.

Abiding in Jesus Christ is a continuing commitment. It's a daily commitment. Jesus said, "If any man will be my disciple, he must take up his cross daily and follow me." First John 2:9 says, "He that saith he abideth in Him ought himself also to walk, even as he walked." If we want to be abiding in Jesus Chirst, we should walk in the manner that He walked. This is what the Bible means when it says to *walk* in the Spirit so that we will not fulfill the lusts of the flesh. It means that we are to advance in our relationship with God. We are to change and grow, becoming more and more like Him.

If you have been a Christian for the last two years, you should be able to look back and see a definite growth in your relationship with the Lord. If you do not seem any closer to Jesus, something is really wrong.

Dropping the Habitual Sins

First John 3:6 says that whoever abides in Christ does not continually and habitually sin. If you are abiding in Him as He desires you to do, you won't willfully commit the same sin over and over again in a premeditated manner. The Bible tells us, "If we confess our sins, He is faithful and just to forgive us our sins, and to cleanse us from all unrighteousness" (1 John 1:9). The word "confess" means to agree with God about your sin. If you agree with God that your sin is wrong, you will also have a hatred for it and you will not have a desire to go out and commit it again. That is true confession.

Many times people confess sin not because they really hate it but because they were caught and were ashamed. But then they go back and do it again. If we are guilty of that, then we are not truly confessing our sins. If we want to abide in Jesus Christ we need to make a commitment to Him: "Lord, by Your strength help me not to go out and commit any sins over and over again." When abiding in Him we receive His spiritual life-giving power, which helps keep us from sin. We have a wonderful promise that when He appears we will have confidence and not be ashamed at His coming (1 John 2:28).

Obeying God Daily

Jesus tells us in John 15:10, "If ye keep my commandments, ye shall abide in my love, even as I have kept my Father's commandments, and abide in His love." Another way to abide in the Lord is to *keep His commandments.* If we say we love God but then break His commandments, this is a double standard. God asks us to demonstrate our love not just by words but by *actions.*

In a marriage relationship a husband expects his wife to be faithful, and she expects the same of him. They demonstrate their love not only by words but by actions. If a husband were to come to His wife and say, "I love you, Honey," and then slap her in the face and throw something at her, she would have a right to question the validity of his commitment. In fact, every time he told her he loved her she would probably duck in fear of some danger coming her way!

In the same way, if we tell the Lord that we love Him, we must also demonstrate our love by the way we live and the actions we take.

Jesus tells us in John 15:11, "These things have I spoken unto you that my joy might remain in you, and that your joy might be full." Abiding in Christ produces a great joy because we're fulfilling the purpose for which God created us. So let's sink our roots deep into Jesus Christ. Let's allow His Holy Spirit to work in our lives by cleansing us and pruning us back so that we might bring forth lasting fruit that is pleasing to God.

Chapter
7

7
Revival Till He Comes

The purpose of this chapter is to talk about the hope of revival for our country, the United States of America. It is my firm belief that judgment is coming to our country as well as to the entire world. A revival does not mean that judgment will never come; it simply means that, at best, judgment is postponed so that more people can come into a life-changing relationship with Jesus Christ. But judgment is coming.

The Enemies Within

The greatest enemies of America are not without but within. Our country is rotting spiritually inside as a result of the abundance we have. It is interesting to note that the sins that caused Sodom and Gomorrah to fall are very similar to the sins of our nation today.

Billy Graham said that if God does not do the same to America as he did to Sodom and Gomorrah, He owes those cities an apology. As Ezekiel 16:49 says, "Behold, this was the iniquity of . . . Sodom: . . . pride, overabundance of food, and idleness." These are the very sins that we see in abundance in America today.

One of our worst sins is our pride—thinking that we are the strongest and the greatest. Our pride has been humbled somewhat in the last ten years or so through incidents like the Vietnam War, Watergate, hostages in Iran, etc. But we're still a very proud nation.

Overabundance of food was another sin of Sodom and Gomorrah. They actually had too much. Though we are not one of the largest nations in the world, we consume a much larger proportion of food than anyone else. Our government has warehouses full of food while people go hungry even in our own country.

Idleness means that people have too much spare time. The real thing that happened to Sodom and Gomorrah was an inward rotting, and that is also the greatest enemy in America today—not Communism, and not enemies from other countries, but the moral and spiritual rotting that is taking place inside our nation today.

There is no doubt that God will judge America. It is not a question of whether He will or won't. It's inevitable: Judgment is coming. Scripture says that righteousness exalts a nation but iniquity brings it down. History has proven this truth over and over again. Where are the great empires of Egypt, Babylon, Greece, Rome, etc.? They seemed indestructible, yet today they are gone. If revival doesn't come, and our people refuse to repent, this nation's judgment will just be a matter of time.

The Future of America

As we study prophecy, we can narrow down the possibilities for the future of America. Many of the great nations of the world are mentioned in the last-days prophecies. We know what's going to happen to China. We know what's going to happen to Russia. We know what's going to happen to Israel. We even know what's going to happen to nations like Turkey, Germany, and Iran. But Scripture is strangely silent on the destiny of America. So what will happen to the United States?

America could possibly become linked to the Common Market. The Bible teaches that in the last days there is coming a world leader who is referred to as the Antichrist. I believe that this leader may come out of the nations of the European Common Market, the ten nations that are in Europe now, daily gaining economic and political strength. One day these ten nations will be the strongest political force on the face of the earth.

It seems possible that, in the last-days scenario, the United States will become partners with the Common Market. There is an organization in existence right now called the Trilateral Commission. Its purpose is to tie the United States and Japan together with the Common Market, encouraging a new monetary system for the world. If this happens, the United States will be an ally, of sorts, with the Antichrist. The U.S. will be working with the Common Market, obviously declining at that point as a world power, and just being one of the partners of the new leader, the Antichrist.

Another Possibility

Another possibility for the U.S. is a nuclear confrontation which we might lose. We could enter into a nuclear war or some kind of war with one of the other nations, perhaps Russia, and lose that war, resulting in the end of the United States as a world power.

There is one other possibility that I want to mention, and this is the one that I hope is true. There could be a massive revival in America, with the Spirit of God moving in a mighty way and thousands and thousands of people coming to a life-changing relationship with Jesus Christ. Then, when the Lord comes back for His church and removes it to be with Himself, it will result in so many people being gone that there will not be enough people left for America to play an important role in the world.

This chapter is written to give hope of the possibility of a revival in our country. The Bible tells us about a young man named Josiah whom God raised up to be the king of Israel during one of their lowest moments of sin (very similar to the conditions of our country today). He led his country into a great revival. As we look at the steps that Josiah undertook for revival, we find that these are the steps that can bring revival to America as well as to you and me personally.

The Right Kind of Revival

Legislating laws that ban abortion, pornography,

etc. does not necessarily produce a spiritual revival. Having a coalition that helps clean up television and put on programs that are more wholesome and family-oriented is not necessarily spiritual revival. Though you might classify these as *moral* revival, they are not *spiritual* revival. But a moral revival will not save our nation; it must be a *spiritual* revival in which we turn back to the living God—one in which we turn back to a personal relationship, individually, with Jesus Christ.

There are many moral, good, upstanding people who, frankly, are on their way to hell. Living morally will *not* get us to heaven, though this is a commendable virtue. Only when we submit ourselves to Jesus Christ as God's provision for our sins can we have eternal life. The Bible tells us in Titus 3:5 that it is "not by works of righteousness which we have done, but according to His mercy [that] He saved us."

Revival is a change of heart. It starts with individuals. The first thing that must be done for revival to come to our country is that you and I must experience a personal revival. The word "revive" actually means "flourish anew." That's what we need to do—to flourish anew spiritually. Jeremiah 6:16 puts it this way: "Thus says the Lord, 'Stand by the ways, and see and ask for the ancient paths, where the good way is, and walk in it; and you shall find rest for your souls' " (NASB).

Perhaps you can look back in your life as a Christian and see that there was a time when your walk with Jesus Christ was much closer than it is today. If so, you need a revival. Perhaps you need to ask for the old paths where the good way is, and to walk there again and find rest for your soul.

Step One to Revival

The first step that Josiah took to bring revival to the nation was to issue a decree that the people were to rebuild the temple. Up to this point in Israel the temple had been pretty much lying in ruins. No one was taking time for God. So the first step to revival was rebuilding the temple.

For us this does not mean rebuilding an actual building, but it means rebuilding our lives. First Corinthians 6:19,20 tells us, "Know ye not that your body is the temple of the Holy Spirit which is in you, which ye have of God, and ye are not your own? For ye are bought with a price: therefore glorify God in your body." We need to rebuild the temple of our life. We need to rebuild ourself spiritually, putting spiritual things as our number one priority.

If you want to find out what kind of priority spiritual things play in your life, make a list of how much time you spend on the various pursuits in your life. How much time do you spend getting yourself ready in the morning? How much time do you spend putting on your makeup? How much time do you spend on your hobbies and your pleasures? Compare this with how much time you spend in prayer. Perhaps you will see that you need to rebuild the temple of your life. You need to once again start serving the Lord with fervor.

A very important thing in rebuilding this temple of our lives is regular fellowship with other Christians. We must be careful not to neglect the assembling of ourselves together. It is crucially important that we spend time with other believers in order to grow in our relationship with Jesus Christ.

Returning to the Word

The second thing that helped bring revival to the land of Israel during Josiah's time was that, as they were rebuilding the temple, they found (almost by accident) the Word of God hidden away somewhere. As they were putting the temple back in order, someone rediscovered the Book of God's law, probably the book of Deuteronomy. So they brought the book to Josiah and read to him what God had decreed for the people to live by. Josiah quickly realized that they had neglected the Word of God.

Many times the Word of God can be lost in our churches today. In many pulpits today the sermons are not centered on the Word of God. To see this illustrated, just pick up the religious section of your local newspapers and read some of the titles of the sermons to be given on the following Sunday. You'll read titles like "Successful Living," "Turn Your Scars into Stars," and "How to Prosper Financially,"—all "successful living" themes. How often do you see titles such as "Living a Life of Repentance," "Denying Yourself," or "Giving Everything to God?" These are the things that require something of us rather than promise the easy life as a Christian.

We need to return to the Word of God, as the people did during Josiah's reign. Hosea 4:6 tells us, "My people are destroyed for lack of knowledge;

because thou hast rejected knowledge, I will also reject thee."

Changed by the Word

When Josiah heard the words of the law read to him, he began to weep as he realized how far short he had fallen from God's expectations. It is not enough to just return to the Word of God; we must let the Word of God change us. The greatest sin is not that the world doesn't hear the Word of God, but that the believers, hearing the Word of God, don't keep it.

Allow God's Word to affect you. Hebrews 4:12 describes the Word of God as sharper than any two-edged sword. It tells us that the Word is a discerner of the thoughts and intents of the heart. As we hear or read God's Word it may hurt a little because God points out to us areas in our lives that need to be changed. We might resist His will because it is something that we just don't want to do, but it is vital that we obey the Word of God, or else we just become well-educated fools.

As Josiah heard the Word of God, it so affected him that he repented. This is the answer that will really bring revival to our nation. In addition to rebuilding the temple, putting spiritual things first in our lives, and returning to the Word of God, we need to repent. Acts 3:19 says, "Repent . . . and be converted, that your sins may be blotted out, when the times of refreshing shall come from the presence of the Lord."

True Repentance

"Repent" is a word that sometimes scares people, but the word simply means to turn around or change our ways. There is a conditional promise that God gives us in Acts 3:19: "If we repent, times of refreshing shall come from the presence of the Lord." The word "refreshing" literally means "cooling and reviving with fresh air." God greatly desires to revive us and refresh us, but it is on the condition that we walk in the ways laid out in His Word.

Perhaps, like Josiah, you realize that your life is not pleasing to God. If so, you too need to repent, or else there is no hope of receiving the blessings that God gives to those who follow Him.

After Josiah learned that God wanted him to turn his life around, we read that he went on to purge the nation of Israel. His first task was to cleanse Israel of idolatry. He tore down all the temples of the pagan gods and no longer allowed them in the kingdom. It is important to know that idolatry is not just bowing prostrate before some idol; idolatry is allowing anything to take the place of God in our lives. It could be a person, a relationship, or even a possession. Some people's idols are their cars. Whenever you look at them, they are cleaning or shining up their car. As believers we must remain on guard that nothing and no one separates us from our relationship with God.

Evil Fantasies?

Ezekiel in the eighth chapter of his book tells us that he was caught up by the Spirit into Jerusalem and was shown an insight into the mind and attitude of the people, even the spiritual leaders of the land. He saw that the people's minds were continually filled with ungodly thoughts and that their imaginations were displeasing to God. Ezekiel was caught up into the temple in Jerusalem, but the New Testament tells us that *we* have become the temple of God and now have the Spirit of God dwelling inside us.

As the Holy Spirit looks into our minds today, I wonder if He finds the same kinds of things that Ezekiel found when he was caught up by the Spirit into the temple in Jerusalem. I wonder if the Lord finds evil imaginations in *your* mind—evil fantasies, wanting to do things that He tells you not to. You justify it to yourself by saying, "Well, at least I don't actually do it." But the truth of the matter is that as you do it in your heart you are disobeying the Lord. Jesus warned us that not only is the committing of the act wrong, but the thinking and desiring are wrong also.

Too Lax in Our Attitudes

The reason that the Israelites had all those images in their temple and all those ungodly influences is because they didn't obey the Lord in the first place. When God brought them into the promised land, He told them to destroy the heathen inhabitants of the land. But they didn't do that; instead, they compromised with the inhabitants and their sins, and now those very sins were coming back to haunt them. In other words, *compromise* was one of the

Israelites' major problems.

We as Christians can also be too compromising, too lax in our attitudes. Adultery is now called an *affair*. Homosexuality is now called *gay*. Within the church is now a great toleration of things that are openly displeasing to the Lord. Sometimes we even boast of how tolerant we are, as though that is a sign of spiritual maturity!

Paul wrote to the church in Corinth, "Your glorifying is not good. Know ye not that a little leaven leaveneth the whole lump? Purge out therefore the old leaven, that ye may be a new lump, as ye are unleavened. For even Christ our passover is sacrificed for us: therefore let us keep the feast, not with old leaven, neither with the leaven of malice and wickedness, but with the unleavened bread of sincerity and truth (1 Corinthians 5:6-8). Paul was exhorting that church not to tolerate people who were openly and blatantly living in disobedience to the Lord. In Romans 12:9 Paul wrote, "Abhor that which is evil [loathe all ungodliness]; cleave to that which is good."

I'm not saying that we as Christians should go out on a crusade of "sin-suffering" and "flesh-finding" in an attempt to be God's spiritual policemen in the church. What I'm saying is that we as believers should do some serious searching into our own lives and ask ourselves if we are allowing compromise to enter our lives. If we allow this compromise to go deep within, we will find that compromise leads to apathy, which in turn leads to spiritual sterility. In other words, we no longer care about ourselves, we no longer care about the church, and we no longer care about the world around us. We become like unsavory salt, which, Jesus said, has no value at all. We become people who are not fulfilling what God created us to do. This is why we must take time to look at ourselves and bring our lives back into submission to the Lordship of Jesus Christ.

Paul wrote in 1 Corinthians 9:27 that he was careful when he preached to others that he himself would not become a castaway or a hypocrite. He wrote that he kept himself under subjection; he watched himself. He disciplined himself and made sure his walk was in accordance with his talk—in other words, that he practiced what he preached. If we watch ourselves and stay within those divine limitations, we can be people whom God wants to use.

Revival Now

God wants to revive you right now. He wants you to come to Him and admit to Him that you have fallen short, that you are not being what you could be as His follower. Psalm 85:6 tells us, "Will You not revive us again, that Your people may rejoice in You?" Let that be your prayer right now—that God would revive you. Do you want to see a revival in your country? Do you want to see a revival in your church? Then revival must start with *you*. *You* must come to the Lord and follow the principles described in this chapter, then ask God to help you apply them personally in your own life.

One word of warning: Now that you have read these things and understand God's expectations of you, if you do not do them, you are in a worse position than if you had never heard them at all. Knowledge brings responsibility. Now that you have knowledge in these areas, apply it and be the person that God wants you to be. Be revived!

Chapter
8

8
Power Till
He Comes

As we seek to occupy until Christ comes and fulfill the things that Jesus asked us to, we realize very quickly how much we need the power of God's Holy Spirit. In the book of Philippians we are told to "work out our own salvation with fear and trembling" (2:12). In other words, God is telling us that as believers we need to bring to completion the things that we have started as a follower of Him in order to live our Christian lives to maturity.

Paul then goes on to say, "For it is God that works in you both to will and to do of His good pleasure" (2:13). How does God do this working in us of His will and His good pleasure? He does it through the power of His Holy Spirit.

Filled with the Spirit
Speaking of the last-days believers, Paul exhorts us in Ephesians 5:16 that we need to redeem the time because the days are evil. As mentioned

earlier, the word "redeem" means to make wise and sacred use of every opportunity. So Paul continues, "Wherefore be not unwise, but understanding what the will of the Lord is" (Ephesians 5:17). As we realize that we are to be making sacred and wise use of every opportunity we need to understand what the will of God is for us in these last days.

What is the will of God? Paul gives us the answer in the next verse: "Be not drunk with wine, wherein is excess, but be filled with the Spirit" (Ephesians 5:18). God is not merely requesting us to be filled; He is *commanding* us to be filled as a father speaks to a son.

In Greek the verb for "filled" is in the present tense, indicating that it is something we should be doing *continually*. It could be translated "Be being filled with the Holy Spirit."

Also, this verb is plural, meaning that it is addressed to *every* person— to all pastors, to all deacons, to all mothers and fathers, to all husbands and wives, to every person.

Finally, this verb is passive, meaning that it is not something we work ourselves into, but *simply receive*. We open our hearts and ask the Lord to fill us with the Spirit. Then we believe He has done so, for Jesus declared that the Father would give His Holy Spirit to all those who ask Him. Thank God that we don't have to work ourselves into an emotional state to receive the power of the Holy Spirit in our lives! Sometimes He touches us emotionally, but other times He does not. But if we ask Him to touch us in this power, we can be confident that He does so as we believe His Word by faith.

Not Left As Orphans

In John 14:15-18 Jesus said, "If you love me, keep my commandments. And I will pray the Father, and He shall give you another Comforter, that He may abide with you forever, even the Spirit of truth, whom the world cannot receive, because it seeth Him not neither knoweth Him; but ye know Him, for He dwelleth with you and shall be in you. I will not leave you comfortless: I will come to you."

Jesus was speaking to the disciples prior to the day of Pentecost. He was telling them that He would not leave them without comfort. It is noteworthy that the word He uses for "comfortless" means "orphans." "I will not leave you as orphans, but I will come to you."

When the founder of Buddhism was bidding his followers farewell he said, "You must be your own light." When Socrates was about to take his fatal cup a disciple said, "You'll leave us orphans." But Jesus, rather than leave us to be our own light or leave us as orphans, promised that His Holy Spirit would come and comfort us and would minister to us and strengthen us: "The Comforter, who is the Holy Spirit, whom the Father will send in my name, He shall teach you all things, and bring all things to your remembrance" (John 14:26).

The Power of the Spirit

The Holy Spirit will teach us and lead us into all truth. Even in the reading of Scripture we need the Holy Spirit to open our eyes: "Open my eyes, that I might behold wonderful things out of Your law!"

(Psalm 119:18). It is so much easier to understand Scripture when its Author takes us by the hand and leads us through it.

We also need the power of the Spirit in our prayer life. Many times we are frustrated in prayer and don't feel like we are really communicating with the Lord the way we should. Yet Romans 8:26 tells us, "The Spirit will help our infirmities." Literally, He will take hold with us when we do not know what we should pray for; the Spirit Himself will make intercession for us with groanings which cannot be uttered.

Sharing Through His Power

We also need the power of the Holy Spirit to effectively share Jesus Christ. The disciples were told to go into Jerusalem and wait for the power of the Holy Spirit to come upon them. Jesus told them in Acts 1:8, "You shall receive power after the Holy Spirit is come upon you; and you shall be witnesses unto me in Jerusalem, and in all Judea, and in Samaria, and to the uttermost part of the earth."

"Witness" in the Greek is the word from which we get our English word "martyr." Jesus was saying that after the Spirit came upon them they would have the power to become martyrs for Him if necessary. Jesus is not necessarily calling you to *die* for Him right now, but He *is* calling you to *live* for Him. He's asking you to let His Holy Spirit give you the strength and boldness and courage to speak up for Him.

If ever there was a time when we need to see the moving of the Holy Spirit in our lives, it is now. So many people have come to church looking for some evidence of God being alive on earth today but have left disillusioned. Rather than seeing a church that is alive and powerful in the Spirit, they find dead orthodoxy. They find empty rituals and traditions, and they hear stories of miracles that were done 2000 years ago in some distant land, but not in their own neighborhood. People need to see that God is alive and working today.

God's Gifts in Action

If ever there was a time that we need to see the gifts of the Holy Spirit in action, it is today. But we must realize that the gifts of the Spirit must operate on the basis of the Word of God. If we cannot find a scriptural evidence for the operation of gifts of the Spirit, then those gifts cannot be right. The Bible tells us that all things should be done decently and in order.

In Ephesians 4:11-16 God tells us that the reason He gave us such gifts as prophet, evangelist, and pastor/teacher is so the church can grow up. These gifts were given "for the perfecting of the saints, for the word of the ministry, for the edifying of the body of Christ, till we all come in the unity of the faith, and of the knowledge of the Son of God, unto a perfect man, unto the measure of the stature of the fullness of Christ; that we henceforth be no longer children, tossed to and fro, and carried about with every wind of doctrine, by the sleight of men and cunning craftiness, whereby they lie in wait to deceive" (Ephesians 4:12-14).

If the gifts of the Holy Spirit are in operation in your life the way God wants them to be, rather than causing you to be unstable and walking around with your head in the clouds, they will actually bring stability into your life as you see God confirming His Word for you personally.

Receiving the Gifts

The way we can receive gifts of the Spirit is laid out for us in Romans 12:1-3, in which Paul says, "I beseech you, therefore, brethren, by the mercies of God, that you present your bodies a living sacrifice, holy, acceptable unto God, which is your reasonable service. And be not conformed to this world, but be transformed by the renewing of your mind, that you may prove what is that good and acceptable and perfect will of God. For I say, through the grace given to me, to every man among you, not to think of himself more highly than he ought to think, but to think soberly, according as God hath dealt to every man the measure of faith." The rest of this chapter talks about the various gifts of the Spirit available to the believer.

The way to receive these gifts is to present yourself to God as a living sacrifice. The sacrifices of the Old Testament were always dead, but God wants us to offer ourselves to Him alive, to offer our entire personality to Him, which is the reasonable or logical thing to do. We're also told that we are not to be conformed to this world, but instead to be transformed as our mind is changed.

One of the major things that God's Holy Spirit

wants to do in our life is to give us a good cleansing of the mind. We hear a lot of talk today about brainwashing and how bad it is. Yet I think a lot of believers could use a good brainwashing of the brain, not in the sense of losing all their faculties and ability to reason, but rather having their minds cleansed from all the ungodly influences taken in over the years.

Our True Selves

We are also told that we should not think of ourselves more highly than we ought to think. We must have a realistic view of ourselves. The person who sees himself as someone great and without flaw is a person who does not see himself realistically. The best way to see ourselves as we really are is to see God as *He* really is. If we see Him in His majesty and in His glory, we'll have no problem seeing ourselves as we really are. Having a humble attitude is an absolute essential for having God's Spirit move through us. James tells us, "God resists the proud, but gives grace to the humble" (4:6). In 1 Peter 5:6 we read, "Humble yourselves under the mighty hand of God, that He may exalt you in due time."

When God called various people in the Bible they were always amazed that God would use them. When the Lord called David, he responded with "Who am I, and what is my life, that You should call me?" When the Lord spoke to Moses through the burning bush he said, "I am not eloquent or a man of words; I am slow of speech." When God called Gideon to deliver the children of Israel from the Midianites, he said "O Lord, how shall I rule Israel? My family is poor and I'm the least of my father's house."

God would bypass any person who said, "Well, it's about time you got around to using me, Lord! After all, I'm talented, charismatic, and good-looking." God uses the person who thinks realistically of himself as God has dealt him a measure of faith.

Opening Our Hearts

Let's open our hearts to the power of the Holy Spirit in our lives so we can be more effective for the Lord. Let's allow the Spirit to work in our personal lives so our understanding of Scripture will grow, our prayer life will deepen, and our witness for Jesus Christ will be strong. Let's open our hearts to be used of God in these last days to allow His Spirit to work through us in the various gifts that he gives.

Chapter
9

9

Heaven's Effect on Earthly People

Heaven!

This is our hope as we await the coming of Jesus Christ. He is not coming just to take us into some obscure oblivion, but He is coming to take us to be with Himself in a place called heaven. As Jesus was preparing to leave His disciples He said, "Let not your heart be troubled; ye believe in God, believe also in me. In my Father's house are many dwelling places; if it were not so, I would have told you. I go to prepare a place for you. And if I go and prepare a place for you, I will come again and receive you unto myself, that where I am, there ye may be also" (John 14:1-3). Jesus was talking about the hope that the disciples had ahead of them when they would join Him in heaven. As a result their hearts didn't need to be troubled.

The same is true for us as last-days believers alive in these perilous times. As we see our world shaking at the seams and much of our security on earth threatened, we realize that we have a hope beyond life on this earth. We have a heavenly hope, where we will be with Jesus for all eternity! He has prepared a place for us.

Our Time Is Short

The longer we live on this earth the more we realize how short our time is here. We realize that, as the Bible says, our life is just a vapor of smoke that appears for a moment and then vanishes away. As the Psalmist writes, our frame is as dust and our days are as grass. A thousand years in God's sight are as a watch in the night. So we need to number our days that we might apply our hearts to wisdom.

It really comes down to realizing that life in this human frame is very temporary. The older we get the more we realize how limited this human body is. Though people do everything conceivable to try to make the body eternally youthful (they get facelifts and dye their hair or try to dress youthfully), they all realize that ultimately the body is going to pass away.

But Jesus said, "I have prepared a place for you; I have a new body that I have fashioned for you, and a new place where you will dwell." The more we live in this earth, the more we become homesick for the return of Jesus Christ, so He will take us to be with Him in heaven.

An exciting thing to realize about heaven is that Jesus really wants us to join Him there! Jesus revealed this in His prayer recorded in John 17. He prayed, "Father, I will that they also whom Thou hast given me *be with me where I am,* that they may behold my glory which Thou hast given me" (verse 24).

A Place of Joy

What is it going to be like when we get to heaven? We know that it's going to be a place with no sadness at all. Revelation 21:4 says, "God shall wipe away all tears from their eyes; and there shall be no more death, neither sorrow, nor crying, neither shall there be any more pain; for the former things are passed away." Not only is heaven going to be a place with no sadness, but it's going to be a place of joy, for Psalm 16:11 tells us, "In Thy presence is fullness of joy; at Thy right hand there are pleasures for evermore." It's hard for us to fathom even in our wildest imagination how wonderful heaven is really going to be.

In 2 Corinthians 12:2-4 Paul described an experience in which he actually went to be with the Lord in heaven. (Many Bible interpreters believe that this happened to Paul when he was stoned during one of his times of preaching.) Paul's spirit left his body and went into the presence of God. As he went into the presence of God and realized that he was in heaven, can you imagine how joyful he felt? No more would he have to go through the persecutions, stonings, rejections, and harassment that he had gone through as an apostle. Now he was in the presence of God forever. I'm sure his heart was ecstatic.

The Paradise of Heaven

But Paul's spirit came back to his earthly body
again. When he later spoke of this experience he
said that he was caught up into paradise and heard
unspeakable words which it is not lawful for a man
to utter (2 Corinthians 12:4). It is fascinating to note
the word that Paul used in this verse for paradise. It
is a word that means "a royal garden of the king,
with all kinds of fruits and flowers." Paul picked the
most beautiful and ecstatic thing he could think of to
describe the presence of God. And the day is coming for us as believers when we will go to be with the
Lord in this wonderful place, never to be separated
from Him again.

In Revelation chapter 4 the Apostle John speaks
of his experience of going into heaven. As he was
caught up in the Spirit he looked on the throne of
God and saw a deep red, a diamond-like hue, a
rainbow going around the throne. Then John
describes how in heaven all the angels and all the
saints are continually worshiping and praising the
Lord.

That's what we look forward to as believers. We'll
be given brand-new, glorified bodies far superior to
the bodies that we live in now. The Bible declares,
"When this corruptible shall have put on incorrup-
tion, and this mortal shall have put on immortality,
then shall be brought to pass the saying that is written, Death is swallowed up in victory. O death,
where is thy sting? O grave, where is thy victory?" (1
Corinthians 15:54,55). Christ will give us brand-
new bodies fashioned like His own resurrection
body, and we'll continually be in His presence.

How We Should Live

Realizing all of these things, how should we live here on earth? The Bible tells us that this prospect should definitely affect the way we live from day to day. You've probably heard the expression "Some people are so heavenly-minded that they're no earthly good." I would suggest that some people are so earthly-minded that they're no heavenly good! I think that if we're really heavenly-minded we'll also be of great value on this earth because we will live our life in a way that is pleasing to God.

In Colossians 3 we have an outline of heaven's effect on earthly people. We're told in this chapter how we should be living as we wait for the coming of the Lord with the anticipation of joining Him in heaven. Colossians 3:1,2 tells us, "If ye then be risen with Christ, seek those things which are above, where Christ sitteth on the right hand of God. Set your affection on things above, not on things on earth."

As we realize that we are risen with Christ, we should have our minds set on heavenly things. The wording "set your affection" could also be translated "set your mind to." So the Scripture is not only telling us to *seek* heaven but to *think* heaven. This doesn't mean that we look at all earthly things as evil in themselves, but only that when we compare them with heavenly things they definitely take a second place.

The Right Attitude

One way to tell if we are truly heavenly-minded is if we can say with Paul, "In whatever state I am, I can be totally content." Are you content where you are today, or are you saying, "Well, I would be content if I could get this new house, or I would be content if I could get married, or I would be content if I could get that raise in pay?"

God wants us to find our contentment not in our circumstances on earth but in our relationship with Him. Paul was well-qualified to say what he did because he had been in both the prisons and the palaces of Rome. He knew what it was like to live well and he knew what it was like to suffer. Yet he said, "I am always content." That's why Paul wrote in 1 Timothy 6:6, "Godliness with contentment is great gain."

Dead to Selfish Me

Colossians 3:2 says, "For ye are dead, and your life is hid with Christ in God." What does it mean to be dead? It means that when we become followers of Jesus Christ and come into a state of being heavenly-minded, we have to let go of our old lives; we have to let go of those things that hold us back spiritually. As Hebrews 12:1 puts it, we need to "lay aside every weight and the sin that so easily besets us."

When Jesus gave the call of discipleship He emphasized the importance of denying self, taking up the cross, and following Him. Jesus is calling us to live a crucified life. This means that we have died to our own desires and our own goals and are living to God. It means that we have said to God, "Not my will but Thine be done." We are willing to do what He says, no matter what He asks.

The Battle and the Glory

Colossians 3:4 says "When Christ, who is our life, shall appear, then shall ye also appear with Him in glory." This is a great hope for us as believers: When Christ returns back to the earth we'll be coming back with Him. We'll be the privileged people who are part of Christ's army as He returns at the second coming.

Verse 5 continues, "Mortify therefore your members which are upon the earth." The word "mortify" means "to put to death and to deprive of power" those things that would keep us away from our relationship with Christ. Every believer realizes that there is a constant battle with the old nature that still wants to go the way of sin. As a Christian, you're either progressing or regressing. You're either building up that new man that God has put in you spiritually or you're building up that old man that is still wanting to live a sinful life.

Cultivating the new man is much like cultivating a fine flower. It takes work. It takes effort. You can't just throw the seed in the ground and let nature take its course. You need to care for that flower and make sure that the snails don't get it and make sure that it's properly watered and fertilized and getting the right amount of sun and shade. Weeds, however, seem to grow without any effort at all. They grow just about anywhere. You see them in dirt fields with no water. You see them coming out of cracks in sidewalks. You really don't have to do anything to help a weed to grow; leave it alone and it will go rampant.

That's like our old nature versus our new nature.

To cause our new nature to grow takes effort. We need to stay close to the Lord in fellowship and we need to cultivate that new nature through study of the Scripture and through prayer. But the old nature doesn't need anything to grow; it grows automatically, like an uncontrollable weed. The best way to put our old nature to death is to give life to our new nature. The best way to deprive our new nature of life is to let our old nature take control. So we are told to put to death and deprive of power those things that would pull us away from our relationship with Christ.

Killing Porneia

Now Paul mentions some of the things that we need to put to death. The first thing he mentions is *fornication*. This word comes from the Greek word *porneia,* which means "illicit sexual relations." (We get our word "pornographic" from this root word.) It includes sexual relationships between single people before marriage, as well as illicit sexual relationships for people who are already married. It also includes homosexuality and other sexual perversions.

Such sins were very prevalent in the culture to which Paul was writing. In fact, in the area of Corinth was a temple to the goddess Aphrodite that had a thousand prostitutes in its employ! So the believers there were constantly being tempted with the sin of *porneia.*

One of the philosophies of that day was Epicureanism, which taught that the chief end of life was pleasure. (It was very much like the philosophy of hedonism taught today.) The believers were warned to stay away from this. Paul at one point wrote, "This is the will of God, even your sanctification, that you should abstain from fornication" (1 Thessalonians 4:3). We as believers need to be careful because this type of sin will tempt us even after we have given our life to Jesus Christ.

Don't think that as a believer you're above being tempted in this area. One of the great men of the Bible, King David, who had a very strong relationship with God, fell to this sin, and it resulted in much catastrophe. Remember that Scripture tells us, "Let him that thinks he stand take heed lest he fall" (1 Corinthians 10:12).

Paul also mentions *inordinate affection,* which is in the same category as sexual sin, for it means an out-of-control passion. He also mentions *evil concupiscence,* which means evil desire. So it's not only *committing* the act of the sin that is wrong, but also *desiring to perform that sin.* Many men who would never go out and be unfaithful to their wives have fantasies about this all the time. That's why we need to nip in the bud all such sinful desires and passions. We need to "think heaven" and to set our affections and our minds on things above.

Death to Greed and Anger

Now Paul mentions a different category of sin: *covetousness,* which means the greedy desire to have more. Some people are never satisfied unless they can obtain more and more possessions. They haven't come to that place of contentment in their relationship with God. I read of a Catholic priest who said that, of all the sins he had heard confessed over the years, he had never heard one person confess the sin of coveteousness! Yet the Bible teaches that coveting or the unbridled desire to get something can keep us away from our relationship with God.

Paul also mentions *idoltry*. Idoltry is anything that occupies a supreme place in our heart apart from the living God.

In verse 8 Paul reaches a new category of words. First he mentions *anger*. This word literally means "an abiding, settled, habitual anger that includes in its scope the purpose of revenge." This is not just the normal kind of anger, but is the kind of anger that wants to get back at the person that caused the misery.

Let's say you're driving down the freeway and need to get off at the next exit. You turn on your signal, but just as you start to move over into the far right lane to get off, the driver in that lane speeds up and cuts you off, and you miss the exit altogether. Unfortunately the next exit is not for ten miles. Now that makes you angry. Most people would perhaps honk at that driver or be angry at him for doing that. But the word used here for anger means that you would not just be angry but would follow that man all the way to his house, pull up in his driveway, and punch him or something. That would be an anger that has revenge within its scope. The Bible tells us that this should not be in the child of God. The Bible teaches, "Be angry; and sin not; let not the sun go down on your wrath" (Ephesians 4:26).

Paul next mentions *wrath*, which literally translated means "boiling agitation of feelings resulting in sudden, violent anger." Are you the kind of person who flies off the handle at the drop of a hat? This is something that God wants you to put to death.

Malice is also mentioned. This means "the disposition of animosity toward another person with a desire to injure."

Watching What We Say

We are also told not to *blaspheme*. This does not mean blasphemy against God but blasphemy against another human being. The word means "slander and a destructive speech injuring another person's good name." Do you find yourself blaspheming other people by saying things you know are not true? Do you find yourself being a gossiper? The Bible says, "The words of a talebearer are as wounds that go down to the uttermost parts of the soul" (Proverbs 18:8). We are told that this should not be in the child of God's life.

We are also told to not have *filthy communication*, which means "low and obscene speech." This includes humor that we would term dirty jokes. These are not fitting for us to be doing as we wait for the coming of the Lord in a heavenly-minded attitude.

A Change of Clothing

Colossians 3:8 tells us to put off all these things—like putting off filthy clothes. If you were walking in the forest and a skunk sprayed you all over, you might as well take your clothes and bury them, because it's doubtful that you would ever be able to completely get rid of that scent. You would put off those clothes once and for all. This is the way that we're told to put off all the things that are not fit for the child of God. We're told to put off *all* these things. Sometimes we're willing to draw the line on certain sins but not on others, but the Bible says that we can't be lenient toward *any* sins.

Finally we are told to "put on the new man, which is renewed in knowledge after the image of Him that created him" (verse 10). The new man is not something that we put on and take off like a suit of clothes, but it's a way of life in which we begin to walk in a relationship with God that is pleasing to Him.

Chapter
10

10

Vision Till
He Comes

In the book of Habakkuk the prophet came to the Lord with certain questions that he wanted to ask God. Habakkuk was a believer who had honest doubts, but rather than speak *against* the Lord he spoke *to* the Lord to resolve his conflicts.

His basic question was one that many people are asking today. Perhaps you have even asked it yourself. "Why doesn't God do something about the evil in the world? Why does God continue to allow the unbelievers to prosper and the righteous to suffer?"

How Long, O Lord?

As we look at this world around us, it is a frustrating experience. We think, "Lord, come quickly—bring judgment." We see the gross injustice being done in our judicial system, in which people get away with horrible crimes by paying very minor penalties or none at all. We see the rise of violent crime, with those who are caught not getting much more than a slap on the wrist. We ask along with Habakkuk, "How long, O Lord, until Your judgment comes upon the earth?" We feel like the martyred people in Revelation 6:10, who cry out, "How long, O Lord, holy and true, dost Thou not judge and avenge our blood on them that dwell on the earth?"

We Need a Goal

God tells the prophet Habakkuk to go up to his watchtower and see what God would say in answer to his questions. Habakkuk writes in 2:2,3, "The Lord answered me and said, 'Write the vision, and make it plain upon tablets, that he may run that readeth it. For the vision is yet for an appointed time, but at the end it shall speak, and not lie; though it tarry, wait for it, because it will surely come; it will not tarry.' " God now reveals His vision for the last days. He tells Habakkuk to write down this vision upon tablets.

This is what I think we as Christians need right now—a spiritual vision of what God wants to do. Proverbs 29:18 says, "Where there is no vision the people perish." What does this mean? The word "vision" actually means "the redemptive revelations of God." So without a vision of the redemptive revelations of God, the people perish. This means that we need a goal, a purpose. We need to know where we are going as believers, because if we don't have a goal we won't know what we're headed toward.

God said to Habakkuk, "Write this vision and make it plain on tablets, so that he who reads it may run and proclaim it." In other words, proclaim it fluently and let the people know what I am doing. This is the attitude that we should take as believers who realize that the Lord could come back at any moment. We must carry this vision out and tell the people what the Lord is doing.

The Lord Is Not Tardy

Peter answers the same kind of question: "Why does the Lord delay His coming?" His answer is, "The Lord is not slack concerning His promise, as some men count slackness, but is longsuffering to us, not willing that any should perish, but that all should come to repentance" (2 Peter 3:9). The word used here for slackness is a word that means "tardy." The Lord is not tardy as some men count tardiness.

When I was in elementary school I was often tardy for class. The teacher would say, "Greg Laurie, you're tardy again!" I used to hate that word *tardy*. But the Lord is not tardy in His return. The appointed time that He has chosen to come back is still the same. The only reason that he has not returned yet is because He is not willing that any should perish, but that all should come to repentance. God's real motive in waiting is to bring more people into His kingdom to spend eternity with Him.

Ten years ago many of us prayed, "Lord, come back." But as we look at the many people who have come to know the Lord in the past ten years (perhaps you're one of them), we're thankful that He did not return at that time. Even now we say, "Lord, come quickly," yet we see that he wants to bring many more people to Himself first.

God Is Looking

God is looking for a person whom He can use. In Ezekiel 22:30 he says, "I searched for a man among them who should build up the wall and stand in the gap before me" (NASB). God is looking for a man or a woman who is willing to step out for Him.

In his early days the great evangelist D.L. Moody was sitting in a church when the preacher said, "The world has yet to see what God can do *with, through,* and *by* the man who is wholly and completely consecrated to Him." Moody said, "I'm going to be that man!"

As you read these words, are you willing to answer that call? Jesus told us that all power is given to Him in heaven and earth. He said, "Go ye therefore and teach [or make disciples] of all nations, baptizing them in the name of the Father, and of the Son, and of the Holy Spirit, teaching them to observe all things whatsoever I have commanded you" (Matthew 28:19,20). God wants us to regard those people out there who do not know Him not as our enemies but as people who desperately need to know the Lord. We need to have a true burden for those who do not know Jesus Christ.

If we don't have a true burden for those outside of Christ, that is a sinful attitude, for James 4:17 teaches that to him who knows to do good and does it not, to him it is sin. We need to be like Jesus; we need to see the multitudes with *compassion*. We also need to be like Nehemiah, who came to the broken walls of Jerusalem and wept as he saw those walls that once symbolized protection, salvation, and separation from the world for the people of God. We need to look at the broken walls of people's lives and reach out to them with a compassionate heart.

We want to be people whom God can use. This is really God's order. He uses *people,* not *programs.* There's no more effective way of communicating Christ than *you* sharing with another person what God has done in your life.

The Burden of the Gospel

If a person is truly spending time in fellowship with the Lord, the natural result will be a desire to tell others. It's really just an overflow of the personal filling from the Lord. This will cause a deep concern for those who are not yet believers, because of the truly perilous situation that they're in.

Paul said in 1 Corinthians 9:16, "Woe is unto me if I preach not the gospel!" Many believers would say instead, "Woe is me if I do preach the gospel!" It's something of a necessary duty to them, and, like Jonah, they may speak the words but they dread it while they do it. Paul's burden for the lost was so intense that he said at one point, "I would be cut off myself if Israel could be saved." In other words, Paul would have given up his own eternal life if by doing this his fellow Jews could have come to know the

Lord. Now that's a burden! But many believers today are not even willing to give up five minutes of
their time to reach people who don't know the Lord.
May God give us a vision for the lost. May He help
us to love them with *His* love, to see them with *His*
eyes, and to reach out to them with *His* forgiveness.

How Shall They Hear?

In his letter to the Romans Paul asks, "How shall
they call on Him in whom they have not believed?
And how shall they believe in Him of whom they
have not heard? And how shall they hear without a
preacher? And how shall they preach except they be
sent? As it is written, How beautiful are the feet of
them that preach the gospel of peace, and bring glad
tidings of good things!" (Romans 10:14,15).

It's interesting to note how Paul describes as
beautiful (out in full bloom) the feet of those who
preach the gospel. In connection with the armor that
we as believers need to wear, it's important to have
our feet shod with the preparation of the gospel of
peace. When Paul alluded to the Christian's armor
in Ephesians 6:11-18 he included the footwear of
the Roman soldier. These soldiers wore sandles with
cleatlike spikes on the soles to give them solid
footing as they moved forward up a hill or through
rugged terrain. We need to move out with the good
news as we await the Lord's return. We need to
have our feet shod with the gospel of peace!

God's Vision for You

Looking back on what Habakkuk said, we need to
run with this vision and proclaim it to the people

who do not yet know the Lord. I believe that it is the responsibility of every Christian to go out and share Jesus Christ with the purpose of leading people to the Lord. The reason many of us have never led anyone to the Lord is because we have simply not told people what God can do for them. God asks, "How will they hear unless somebody tells them?"

Not Just a Spectator

God told Habakkuk that he needed a vision. We also need this vision, not only for those who do not know the Lord, but for those who do. God wants to give you a vision not only for the world around you but also for the church you are a part of. I do hope that you are a part of a body of believers. This is so important if we really want to enter into all that God has for us.

In Hebrews 10:24,25 we are told, "Let us consider one another to provoke unto love and to good works; not forsaking the assembling of ourselves together, as the manner of some is, but exhorting one another, and so much the more as ye see the day approaching." We need to realize that the Lord wants us to be actively involved in a body of believers where we are not just a spectator but a participator.

The church is something like a giant football game. There are 60,000 people in the grandstand watching while 22 people do all the work! I heard one person say that the church is like Noah's ark: If it weren't for the storm outside I couldn't stand the stench inside! Many people say, "I don't go to church because it's unsatisfying. I don't get encouraged. I don't get ministered to." I heard one person say, "I can't go to church because there are too many hypocrites in the church." I told him if he ever found the "perfect church" he had better not join it because he would spoil it!

The point is that if you only go to church to be helped and strengthened, you will be dissatisfied. You must go to church not only to receive but also to give. You must adapt what Jesus said in your own life, and go not only to be *ministered to* but to *minister*. You will find that as you share and give out what God has given you, He will bless you as a result. As you give, it will be given unto you, pressed down, shaken together, and running over.

Church is not like a takeout restaurant, an "In-and-Out Chapel" where we can go and then leave without making any commitment or getting to know any people. Find a good church where the Word of God is taught and where people are growing in Him, and where you can be a functioning part, contributing in what God would have you do.

Heaven's Impact

As we wait for the Lord to come back for us, and as we realize the hope that we as believers have for heaven, let's become heavenly-minded people who allow heaven's effect on us to really have an impact. As we await the return of Jesus Christ to the earth, let's occupy till He comes. Let's take the things discussed in this book and really apply them in our lives. By doing this we will be doing what Jesus asked of us when He told us what we ought to be doing as we await His coming.

Greg Laurie is senior pastor of Harvest Christian Fellowship in Riverside, California, which has a weekly attendance of more than 6,000. As a teacher, Greg is heard throughout the United States on his radio program "A New Beginning."

Greg and his wife, Catherine, have a young son, Christopher.

If you would like information on teaching tapes or the radio ministry of Greg Laurie write to:

Harvest Ministries
P.O. Box 4424
Riverside, California 92504